W9-APD-655

THE LIBRARY OF GRAPHIC NOVELISTS™

ART SPIEGELMAN

TOM FORGET

The Rosen Publishing Group, Inc., New York

*To Ma, who read my comics to me when I couldn't read them.*

Published in 2005 by The Rosen Publishing Group, Inc.
29 East 21st Street, New York, NY 10010

**Library of Congress Cataloging-in-Publication Data**

Forget, Thomas.
Art Spiegelman / Tom Forget.
    p. cm. — (The library of graphic novelists)
Includes bibliographical references and index.
ISBN 1-4042-0281-1 (lib. bndg.)
1. Spiegelman, Art—Juvenile literature. 2. Comic books, strips, etc.—
United States—History—20th century—Juvenile literature.
I. Title. II. Series.
PN6727.S6F67 2005
741.5973—dc22

2004011257

*Manufactured in Malaysia*

# CONTENTS

When people imagine American comic art, most visualize the strips that appear in the Sunday newspaper. Others visualize an old stack of comics that disappeared one day after Mom cleaned the closet. These cartoons changed little throughout the years as staple characters like Charles Schulz's *Peanuts* took a philosophical look at life, or as muscle-bound superheroes like Batman beat madmen into submission and saved the citizens of Gotham City. Some people might claim that comics aren't an art form at all, but only a simple form of children's entertainment. Few people expected that the comic book would eventually grow up and embrace topics any more serious than whether Green Lantern would finally capture Sinestro.

Comic books originally emerged during the Great Depression of the 1930s, a time long before television or computers, when

All of the comics in this collection were created in the 1930s. Superman, seen here on an issue of *Action Comics*, was cocreated in 1938 by artist Joe Shuster and writer Jerry Siegel, both from Cleveland, Ohio. The first issue of *Marvel Comics* appeared that same year and featured another superhero, the Human Torch. *Disney Comics*, and its timeless characters such as Mickey Mouse and Donald Duck, began a bit earlier, in 1930, with Walt Disney drawing the first issues entirely by himself.

they represented an inexpensive form of entertainment. Among the early pioneers of comic books were Jewish immigrants, whose families had escaped the horrible wave of anti-Semitism that had swept through Germany and would ultimately culminate in the Holocaust. Comics provided a window into the minds of their creators. Superheroes like Superman and Wonder Woman were also immigrants, not sure how they fit into a new environment. Batman tried to make sense of a world in which his parents could be taken from him without anyone ever having to explain their absence. Stan Lee (Lieber) and Jack Kirby (Kurtzberg) created the X-Men—a group of powerful young people who were hated and feared because they were different.

While the Jewish immigrant experience in America was subtly incorporated into these comics and their stories, it was rare to see these life events portrayed literally. In fact, many of the creators went out of their way to avoid seeming too "Jewish," even changing their names. It would take many decades for comic artists and journalists to start acknowledging the art form's ethnic roots, or to make comics that spoke explicitly of religion or politics.

But editorial content was not the only place where comics were restrained. For decades, the very method of publishing comics was confined almost totally to monthly magazine sales. No one thought to publish a larger book of comics that would not be part of a continuing story. Few people even considered that a stand-alone comic book could be successful.

Graphic novels, as we have come to recognize them, didn't come into existence until the late 1970s, but their popularity has grown ever since. Today, mainstream comic publishers like Marvel and DC continue publishing their monthly books, but they also publish individual stories as trade paperbacks, sold both in comic stores and at national bookstore chains.

Art Spiegelman is an artist who has truly pushed the boundaries of comics in both form and content. A veteran of the comics industry who began drawing professionally in the 1960s, Spiegelman has worked steadily in almost every aspect of the genre. He has written, drawn, painted, edited, designed, and taught over the years, and he is always searching for new horizons. His comic, *Maus*, while originally published in serialized installments, was eventually collected as a graphic novel. Its release shattered people's idea about what comic books were supposed to be. *Maus* brought personal religious identity and politics into global focus in a forum that had previously given voice to superheroes, fantastical creatures, and misfits.

By putting his identity as a Jewish man front and center, Spiegelman was able to honor the comic book's beginnings, and therefore all of the European immigrants who had worked to create the industry. The success of *Maus* helped elevate comics to a platform of serious art, showing people that the comic art form was no longer one reserved solely for young people.

While *Maus* is Spiegelman's most popular and recognized release, it represents just one work within a lifetime of his achievements. Spiegelman has been a tireless promoter of comic art and has fearlessly used it to bring attention to society's problems. For Spiegelman, making comics remains the best way to communicate to people. In his lecture "Comix 101," he says, "comics echo the way the brain works. People think in iconographic images, not in holograms, and people think in bursts of language, not in paragraphs."

# CHAPTER 1

# CHANGING COMICS

**A**rt Spiegelman was born in Stockholm, Sweden, in 1948. His parents, Vladek and Anja (neé Zylberberg) Spiegelman, were Polish Jews who had immigrated to Sweden from German-occupied Poland just after World War II (1939–1945). Spiegelman's parents were survivors of the Holocaust and had spent time during the war in Auschwitz, a Nazi death camp. Although the Spiegelmans were happy and successful in Sweden, they had always dreamed of coming to the United States. Europe held many bad memories for them, including the death of their first child, Richieu, who perished in World War II. Born after the war ended, Art Spiegelman never met his older brother.

Like many Jewish refugees, the Spiegelmans eventually made their way to the United States in the 1950s. They settled in New York City, in the

Rego Park neighborhood of Queens. After arriving in New York, they maintained a lifestyle similar to most other families. Like many American boys, Art was interested in comics. When he was growing up in the 1950s, American comics were diverse. Television was only just becoming available to a mainstream audience, though most people commonly attended movie screenings at their local theater. And while many adults listened to radio broadcasts at home, kids often turned to comics for easily accessible and inexpensive entertainment.

Today's comic enthusiasts are familiar with well-known superheroes like Batman, Captain America, and Wonder Woman, all characters who were popular when Spiegelman was a youngster, but many others also existed. Among the types available were military, horror, romance, and western comics; illustrated classic literature; teen dramas; and science fiction. Great artists like Jack Davis, Gil Kane, Wallace Wood, Jack Kirby, Will Eisner, Alex Toth, and Joe Kubert were among the masters who created the comic art form from the beginning. Few were immediately recognized for their talents.

## Wertham's War

Just as Spiegelman became interested in the variety of comics that were popular throughout the 1950s, the industry came under fire. The future of comics was in jeopardy, largely due to the efforts of Dr. Frederic Wertham, a German American psychiatrist. In 1954, Wertham published a book called *Seduction of the Innocent*, which

New York assemblyman James A. Fitzpatrick (left), chairman of the New York State Joint Legislative Committee to study the publication of comic books, and Republican Senator Robert C. Hendrickson of New Jersey examine some of the more controversial horror comic publications in 1954. At the time, union printers in New York were asked by the Senate Juvenile Delinquency Subcommittee not to print horror comic books based on the opinion that they were morally reprehensible.

alleged that comics were destroying American morals, specifically the morals of young people. Wertham genuinely believed that comics were hurting children. He claimed that Batman was a homosexual fantasy because he lived with Robin, a teenage boy, and he was particularly harsh toward the horror comics published by William Gaines's Entertaining Comics, or EC. Today's critics consider EC's books among the most beautifully

After 1954, magazine distributors often refused to service comic publishers if their issues lacked the Comics Code Authority "seal of approval." In response to the Senate hearings on the "immoral" content of some popular comic books, major comic book publishers joined together to form the Comics Code Authority (CCA). The CCA was created by the publishers to self-censor their own publications.

drawn, intelligent, and sophisticated from the 1950s, but they were undeniably extreme. Specific titles such as *Terror, Weird Science,* and *Vault of Horror* were also singled out as being too graphic or immoral.

Wertham's book led the U.S. government to investigate the comics industry and hold Senate hearings to help determine the art form's impact on the nation's youth. The result of the hearings was the formation of the Comics Code Authority (CCA) in 1954. The CCA regulated the content of comics, and its seal soon appeared on the front cover of every comic book. Under CCA guidelines, criminals always had to be punished; werewolves, vampires, and other supernatural beings could no longer be depicted as characters; and any discussion or illustration of drug use was illegal. The new rules made it virtually impossible for EC to publish the horror comics that were its specialty. It was a terrible blow to the company, but it paved the way for William Gaines, the president of EC, to focus his energy on publishing something that would have the greatest impact on Spiegelman's career: *Mad* magazine.

Publisher William Gaines, seen here in his New York office in 1989, holds a copy of *Mad* magazine. First produced and created by Gaines and editor Harvey Kurtzman, *Mad* became an American institution of humor, and its mascot, Alfred E. Neuman (*background*), an American comic icon.

## Mad About Mad

*Mad* magazine, an off-the-wall humor magazine, was first published by EC in 1952. Many of EC's top horror comic artists simply shifted their energies into *Mad*, making it one of the best-looking magazines on the shelves. *Mad* was full of celebrity satire, parodies of popular movies, and zany pop culture references. Because the jokes were crude and gross (often at the expense of popular advertising campaigns), the magazine immediately became popular with young people. The humor in *Mad* was directed to younger readers' interests and pastimes, much to the chagrin of parents and teachers who believed it offered little improvement over the earlier horror comics. Spiegelman was a huge fan of *Mad*. He was also intrigued that many parents saw the offbeat humor magazine as a threat. In the future, Spiegelman would always attempt to elicit the same provocative reaction from mainstream society.

Today, *Mad* magazine continues to be published, but it is no longer considered the threat to morality that it once was. The kids who made it so popular in the 1950s and 1960s are now middle-aged. But some of them, like Spiegelman, have never forgotten the outrage that *Mad* inspired. When Spiegelman became involved with the alternative comics scene in the late 1960s, *Mad*'s in-your-face attitude would remind him never to shy away from subjects that might make people angry or uncomfortable. In fact, Spiegelman sought them out with intent.

## Stan the Man

After the formation of the CCA and its infamous code, superhero comics also faded away. Superman, Batman, and a few others have survived, but most of the costumed do-gooders who had fought the good fight during World War II and after were no longer being published.

By the early 1960s, despite a small resurgence of superheroes at DC Comics (the publisher of *Superman* and *Batman*) under editor Julius Schwartz, there were few superhero comics being published.

Meanwhile, at Timely Comics, a publishing company that had produced *Captain America*, the *Human Torch*, and *Sub-Mariner* during World War II, a young writer named Stan Lee came up with an idea to make comics that would appeal to teenagers. Timely wanted a new look for its new name, Marvel, so Lee created superheroes that were more like a family than DC's Justice League (a team of successful superheroes with its own books). Lee's characters were called the Fantastic Four, a group of humanlike superheroes who complained, had problems, and fought among themselves. The Thing, Benjamin Grimm, was an air force pilot stuck in the body of an orange rock monster. He was a hero because he had no other choice, not because he wanted to be. Johnny Storm, who was called the human torch, was a moody, hot-tempered teenager who also happened to be able to burst into flames. Reed Richards and Susan Storm, Johnny's older sister, acted as the parents to the group. In any given issue, there was just as much chance that Ben Grimm would start a fight with a member of the family as Dr. Doom or another menace would.

The Fantastic Four was a massive hit. Lee and artists Jack Kirby and Steve Ditko created a cast of heroes with unlikely problems: Iron Man had a heart condition; Hawkeye was mistaken for a criminal; the X-Men were

These two panels are taken from an old Marvel title called *Amazing Fantasy* (1962), which first introduced the character known as Spider-Man. Created by writer Stan Lee and artist Steve Ditko, Spider-Man took to crime fighting in the streets of New York to avenge the death of his uncle. As a bookish high school student named Peter Parker when he wasn't a superhero, Spider-Man, a character who gained his powers after being bitten by a radioactive spider, immediately resonated with young people.

hunted by authorities because of their strange powers; and Mighty Thor's human identity was that of a crippled doctor. The legendary Kirby drew almost all of them, but the greatest and most popular of all the creations was Lee and Ditko's Amazing Spider-Man.

Never had the deck been stacked so heavily against a superhero. Peter Parker, the human identity of Spider-Man, was an orphan who lived with his sickly, aged aunt. He was a brilliant science student but was mercilessly picked on by other students for being poor and a nerd. Nobody liked him as Peter Parker, and the local newspapers attacked his crime-fighting abilities as Spider-Man. But with teenagers, Spider-Man was an incredible hit. For the first time, young people could read about a character who had the same problems as they did.

This new comic revolution, however, came too late for Spiegelman. By the time Marvel Comics had reached the height of its popularity, he was already losing interest in the medium. He followed the Marvel books for the first year. Although Spiegelman was intrigued by the interesting new quirks in the characters, he remained obsessed with satire magazines like *Mad*. In fact, as far as superheroes were concerned, Spiegelman didn't respond to them. "[I was] born out of whatever dimwitted understanding I had of what my parents went through when I was a kid, I was very distrustful of armies, or Boy Scouts, people marching, of team sports, and a lot of the [Jack] Kirby world is involved in working in teams," Spiegelman explained in a two-part interview in *The Comics Journal*, issue numbers 180 and 181.

Spiegelman had begun reading the works of twentieth-century, Austria-Hungary–born Franz Kafka at a young age and was developing a larger interest in the struggles of the individual. He was curious about the strange and interesting things that made a person stand apart from society. Spiegelman wasn't interested in watching teammates get along, but he related to some of the adventures of the lonelier heroes. "So if I was going to have an attraction to superheroes, as far as superheroes have an attraction for me, I was more likely to move into a more alienated world of Spider-Man, or before that, the more alienated world of Batman," he stated in *The Comics Journal*. As his later work would show, Spiegelman claimed that "[The activities of] individuals were more interesting to me than [those of] the larger conglomerate."

Unfortunately for Spiegelman, the Marvel revolution made the comics industry swing all the way to the other side. Instead of superhero comics becoming extinct, they slowly ate up the market. By the late 1960s, mainstream comics almost totally comprised superheroes. But as youth culture changed and that generation of kids went to college, there was an underground developing in the world of comics.

## Underground Rumblings

Spiegelman wasn't alone in his dissatisfaction of the then-current direction of the comics industry. Many artists in the mid- to late 1960s remembered the way things had been before the comics code, when comics weren't so strictly regimented and their subject matter was more diverse. The artistic style of comics, which had once ranged from the lush, elegant turn-of-the-century drawings of Winsor Mckay's *Little Nemo in Slumberland* strip to the dark, inky dynamics of Will Eisner's *The Spirit* of the 1940s to the 1950s cartoon like Donald Duck and Uncle Scrooge, was now dominated by the style of Jack Kirby. Marvel Comics, in particular, used almost all Kirby-inspired artists. By the late 1960s, though, society was changing rapidly, and comics were ready to change, too.

Spiegelman attended the High School of Art and Design in New York City. As soon as he could, he began studying comics seriously. In the mid-1960s, he began working on a comic with African American classmate Ronnie Hamilton. Spiegelman ghostwrote the work *Super Colored Guy* for Ronnie under the name "Artie X," and it appeared in a small Harlem newspaper. Although he was only a teenager, Spiegelman was starting to find his footing as a professional comic-book writer. Race relations were changing in the United States, and Spiegelman's comic work was riding the wave that would break in a few years. It was an early taste of controversial subject matter, but it would not be his last.

Spiegelman's mother and father were hoping that he would become a dentist. As a good, practical profession, it made sense, but writing comics seemed like the only occupation that grabbed Spiegelman's interest. At the end of the decade, he was ready for college. Spiegelman enrolled at Harpur College, and later, the State University of New York (SUNY) at Binghamton, and studied art and philosophy—not exactly subjects that would have prepared him to become a dentist. These interests would later figure heavily into his work.

# CHAPTER 2

# COMIX AND OTHER GROUNDBREAKING WORK

As the 1960s rolled on, the United States was changing rapidly. The comic world was no different. After the incredible success of Marvel Comics's new books, superheroes had become the major force in the industry. The westerns, romances, war comics, and comedies were still around, but now they comprised only a small portion of the market. For the most part, comic books had become big business, and it seemed like there was little room for change or experimentation. If *Spider-Man* comics sold, Marvel was not about to mess with its formula.

While mainstream comics were becoming more formula-driven and conservative, many college students who had been inspired by Marvel comics as teenagers had come to expect something more daring. Even at Marvel itself, there was a glimpse of experimentation. *Dr. Strange*, a Lee/Ditko comic about a magician in New York's hip Greenwich Village, featured journeys into bizarre dimensions. It is credited with heavily influencing underground authors such as Ken Kesey. *Nick Fury: Agent of S.H.I.E.L.D.* was a comic that combined cutting-edge fashion and graphics with the spy craze started by the popularity of James Bond movies.

Young adults of the late 1960s found themselves at the center of a radical cultural landscape, much different than the conservative decades of the 1940s and 1950s. The Vietnam War (1961–1975) was in full swing by the time Spiegelman enrolled in college. The war's impact on his age group, and the entire country, was massive. Students saw young soldiers being sacrificed to a confusing war that many people believed was unnecessary. As a form of escape, young people often turned to rock music for inspiration and as a way to separate them from the older generation. For those who couldn't sing or play an instrument, however, the world of comics represented a way to make their voices heard.

## Comix Zap the World

The conservative attitude of adults in the late 1960s presented a challenge to the students who wanted to take the mainstream world of comics to task. Many teens and twenty-somethings had been raised in households where emotional responses were considered inappropriate and where their ideas were not taken seriously. The loud rock and roll of Jimi Hendrix, Janis Joplin, The Rolling Stones, and The Who made twice as much noise as anyone else and it demanded to be heard. Young comic artists had to find their own way of making noise.

*Mad* magazine's insane popularity in the late 1950s had influenced the ideas of its young readers. The gross humor and oddball parodies of popular culture used in *Mad* made an indelible impression on an entire generation of readers. *Mad*'s founding editor and best-known talent, Harvey Kurtzman, had pushed the limits of humor in its pages, and in his post-*Mad* project, a magazine called *Help!*, he allowed space for amateur artists. Many people who appeared in *Help!* would soon make a larger impact on the world of underground comics. One of them, Robert Crumb, would almost single-handedly start a revolution in the world of comics with the publication of *Zap Comix*.

## Coloring Outside the Lines

Because there were only a handful of comics publishers, however, most of which published material about superheroes, there was very little material available for adults. Society still viewed comic books as an inexpensive entertainment for kids—a medium that distracted youngsters from educational reading and had little to offer. Most people certainly did not consider comics an art form. Many didn't even know that American GIs had been reading comics for decades. Big companies like Marvel, DC, and Gold Key weren't interested in publishing books for adults either, simply because they didn't know if they would sell well.

Crumb was a strange and socially awkward young man. The product of a strict, emotionally restrained household, he and his brothers had few outlets for entertainment. From a very young age, Robert Crumb and his brother Charles were obsessed with comic strips. They spent hours making their own comics for years. By 1967, Robert Crumb had become a truly incredible and original draftsman. Whereas the popular comics of the time were dominated by Kirby's bold, high-contrast style, Crumb drew in a style closer to the comic strips of the 1930s and 1940s. His lines were thinner and scratchier, and he used crosshatching (a technique that uses overlapping and crossing lines to create the illusion of depth) to create shadows.

For his subject matter, Crumb took many of the cutting-edge elements of *Mad* magazine, such as parody, and turned the volume up to eleven. He was obsessed with females, particularly full-figured women, and his comics pictured them in all of their (often naked) glory. Crumb's characters engaged in rude and obnoxious behavior, and his writing was often crass and offensive. Crumb used his comics as a huge clearing house for all of his insecurities and obsessions. He took whatever disturbing thoughts rattled around in his brain and put them down on paper.

Until Crumb, explicit sex acts could only be found in homemade comics and the Tijuana Bibles—crude, illegal

A reprint of Robert Crumb's Zap Comix, issue one, first printed in 1968. According to many comic artists and historians, Crumb, a self-described shy, maladjusted "weirdo," completely reinvented the medium, drawing imagery and writing narratives that were edgy, gutsy, and according to some, offensive. Crumb's name is considered synonymous with the underground comix movement of the 1960s.

comic strips featuring popular characters in sexual situations. Crumb and Spiegelman were but two of the budding comic artists who were influenced by the brewing underground movement. Crumb's comics and characters, such as Mr. Natural and Devil Girl, appealed to people who were excited by that same kind of taboo thrill found in reading the Tijuana Bibles. They featured all the excitement of reading something forbidden and became immensely popular in a short time. Before long, Crumb became a champion in the world of comics for the hippie movement of the 1960s.

## Comix in the Mix

The new underground movement was usually called comix, a name that helped set it apart from mainstream comics. The unusual spelling also helped draw special attention to its artists. (In the past, the letter X had often symbolized the forbidden: Strong alcohol was always pictured with three X's on the bottle; pornography was always rated X; etc.) The name also had a deeper significance. It was Spiegelman himself who claimed that the name "comix" stood for the "co-mixing" of words and pictures.

The world of comix provided hippies, who usually had some artistic interests, with a place to talk about the issues and pastimes that were especially important to them. In no time, there were comix for every political cause and social group. Gays and lesbians, feminists, fundamentalist Christians, and even drug users all started publishing their own comix.

The underground comix scene was mostly concentrated in San Francisco, California, home in 1968 to one of the very first "comics only" stores, the San Francisco Comic Book Company. Until that time, comics were mostly available in drugstores and at newsstands. And businesses often refused to sell something its owners found obscene. Comic stores that sold only comics had the freedom of greater choice in what type of comics they wanted to sell, and the underground comix were free to publish without the CCA seal there.

In this atmosphere of political and artistic freedom, Spiegelman found himself approaching adulthood. Despite his parents' desire for him to find a stable and profitable career in dentistry, he was more interested in literature and philosophy. Many college students at that time were experiencing a freedom that earlier young adults would not have believed. Recreational drug use, especially with marijuana and hallucinogens such as lysergic acid diethylamide (LSD), was becoming more widespread. Many of the comix of that time contained themes surrounding this new counterculture. Spiegelman was dazzled by this freedom and was soon caught up in the same world.

## The Dark Side of the Sixties

While in college, Spiegelman found himself knee-deep in the freedom of campus life in the late 1960s. He began experimenting with LSD, a hallucinogenic drug sometimes referred to as "acid." Spiegelman claimed in a 1997 article in *Mother Jones* that he "had been registered in an upstate New York College, avoiding the draft and taking LSD as casually as some of my contemporaries now drop antacids." During one acid "trip," he began hallucinating wildly and losing control. In his own words, he "woke up in restraint sheets in a state mental hospital. I wasn't sure who or where I was. I was neither male nor female, neither young nor old, neither black nor white. I was, as Popeye or Jehovah might have put it, what I was, and that's all that I was," he said in *Mother Jones.*

This was the beginning of a very dark time for Spiegelman. His one night in the hospital turned into a couple of months, an experience that he later recounted in a comic story called "Breakdowns." While he recovered, Spiegelman was forced to face his personal demons. He had to take stock of his life. After his stay in the hospital, Spiegelman had to return to his parents' house in Queens in New York, as a condition of his release. After living with them for three months, he came home one night in 1968 from a weekend with his girlfriend to find police and a crowd gathering in front of his parents' home. Spiegelman could tell that something was wrong, but he didn't know what. A cousin who was outside took him away and told him that his mother was sick. Soon Spiegelman met with a doctor who told him the sad truth: his mother was dead from an apparent suicide.

## "Prisoner on the Hell Planet"

The suicide was a huge blow to Spiegelman and his father. His mother had been troubled even before the events of World War II. Yet the fact that she took her own life twenty years after the birth of her second son seemed inconceivable. To deal with the pain, Spiegelman turned to his work. In 1973, in *Short Order Comix* number 1, he created an autobiographical comic about the suicide, "Prisoner on the Hell Planet." The autobiographical content was to become a staple in Spiegelman's work, especially during his later years.

At the time of Spiegelman's mother's suicide in 1968, the comix movement was at its height. The underground comix scene gave him a place to pour out his pain and confusion as well as to face his sadness with the kind of satire that he had come to love in *Mad* magazine. During the late 1960s and early 1970s, Spiegelman became a regular contributor to comix of all kinds, including *Real Pulp*, *Young Lust*, and *Bizarre Sex*. In 1971, he moved to San Francisco, placing him at the home of the underground comix movement. San Francisco's scene featured underground artists like Crumb, Spain Rodriguez, Gilbert Shelton, and Rick Griffin. Being in the middle of it all gave Spiegelman the opportunity to work on a variety of titles. He edited or contributed to titles such as *Short Order Comix*, *Bijou*, *Douglas Comix*, and *Sleazy Scandals of the Silver Screen*.

## Arcade

In 1975, Spiegelman co-founded his own comix magazine, *Arcade*, with Bill Griffith, who had been a staple of San Francisco underground comix since the beginning. His comic, *Zippy the Pinhead*, was a politically incorrect comic about a deformed character. *Arcade* gave Spiegelman the opportunities not only to publish

Originally published in *Short Order Comix*, number 1, Spiegelman detailed his mother's tragic 1968 suicide in "Prisoner on the Hell Planet." In these panels, Spiegelman is told of the sad news by the family doctor who did little to soften the blow.

his own work, but to provide a forum for other up-and-coming artists to publish their work. Crumb published his work in *Arcade*, as did S. Clay Wilson and Justin Green.

In many ways, *Arcade*'s publication signaled the end of the first era of underground comix, at least as the period related to the original antiwar cause. Once the Vietnam War ended in 1975, the unity among the pacifist movement lost its momentum. The massive youth culture that had sprung up around it began to fade. Soon, much of the bohemian counterculture audience who had been buying comix turned to other interests. Drawing and writing comics remained in

Short Order, a collaborative comix series created by Art Spiegelman and Bill Griffith in 1973, also featured work by Robert Crumb and Rick Griffin. This cover, the second issue in the series, was designed and drawn by Bill Griffith. Spiegelman had been loosely involved in the underground comix scene since the late 1960s.

Spiegelman's blood, and he continued working in the medium with the same passion as he had before.

## Eisner's Contract

In 1977, as the first wave of underground comix was ending, and mainstream superhero comics continued to churn out issue after issue, one of history's greatest comic book artists had something new up his sleeve. Will Eisner had been working in comics since the 1930s. He was the creator of *The Spirit*, a 1940s comic strip about a crimefighter, who expanded the possibilities of comics more than anyone had before. (That is until Jack Kirby—who studied under Eisner in the Eisner-Iger Studio—came on the scene later in the 1950s).

In *The Spirit*, Eisner introduced the idea of splash pages—full-page illustrations at the beginning of a story that sum up what is happening in the strip and set its mood. He also experimented with typography, making the actual editorial content a part of the picture instead of something that was only placed on top of it. These techniques of visual storytelling were considered vastly ahead of their time, and they are commonly used today. Also, at a time when comics were considered strictly for kids, Eisner took great pains to make *The Spirit* a comic story that could interest adults. He stuffed it with dark shadows, beautiful women, and the hard-boiled violence of a suspense-filled detective movie.

Eisner spent much of his time in the 1940s in the U.S. Army because he was drafted. Later, in the 1960s, he continued doing comic work for the U.S. Army. He went to Vietnam during the conflict to do accurate drawings for an army teaching publication called *Preventive Maintenance Monthly*, where he explained how engines and tanks worked. After the war ended, he gained high-paying work in the advertising industry. In 1977, in his fifth decade creating comics, Eisner released a work called *A Contract with God*. His newest release proved that he had not finished expanding the possibilities of the comic medium.

Until that point, comics were usually released in the familiar monthly magazine format. Eisner had different ideas. *A Contract with God* was released as a single volume. The story was told from start to finish in one book instead of being in serialized monthly comics. Eisner is credited with the development of what is now considered the world's first graphic novel. In an interview, Eisner explained why he came up with the term, claiming that he used it to avoid pitching the story to a publisher as a monthly comic book. He knew that comics had a long reputation of being work that only interested kids, and he wanted to get his foot in the door with a publisher of books for adults.

The format of *Contract* wasn't the only groundbreaking attribute of the book, however. The subject matter was also very different from what people were accustomed to reading. Instead of mainstream superheroes solving crimes, or the underground mix of satirical humor and parody, *Contract* was a story about average people living average lives in a New York tenement. Although Jim Steranko and Gil Kane also

Even though Will Eisner had worked out many of his ideas in a weekly serialized comic called *The Spirit*, he was still reaching for an older audience.
He hoped to capture adults' attention with the 1977 release of the graphic
novel *A Contract with God*. This panel, taken from *Contract*, shows one of
his book's Bronx tenement characters after the death of his daughter
Rachele. Both Eisner and Spiegelman had the similar goal of creating a
broader readership for what they called graphic storytelling.

released similar narrative works around the same time, *Contract* set the stage for serious-minded comic artists who had different stories to tell. Spiegelman, in particular, saw in Eisner's work a similarity to his own. This was the type of creative thinking and execution that particularly interested him. In a speech he delivered in 2002 upon receiving a Lifetime Achievement Award from the National Foundation for Jewish Culture, Spiegelman gave credit to Eisner. "His enduring creation of the 1940s, *The Spirit*, was possibly the first to show the world that these comics weren't just for kids." But before Spiegelman could devote time to the serious business of creating graphic novels, he had a little more *Mad*-style silliness to get out of his system.

# CHAPTER 3

# ART IN
# THE EIGHTIES

Art Spiegelman was a lifelong New Yorker, and in 1975, he returned to his home city after a few years in San Francisco. Once home, he began doing comic illustration work for the *New York Times*, the *Village Voice*, and *Playboy*. Publications such as the *Times* were considered more highbrow, and Spiegelman's work for them signified that comics were starting to be considered more than just kids' entertainment. But in addition to the new work, Spiegelman fell in love.

Françoise Mouly, a native of Paris, France, and a former architecture student and art director, became Spiegelman's wife in 1977. The French, and Europeans in general, have always considered comics more seriously than Americans, so in Françoise, Spiegelman found someone who could share his appreciation for what the French called "the ninth art." After spending the bulk of his career creating comics as well as learning about the history of the medium, Spiegelman began teaching students how to create comics in 1979. The School of Visual Arts (SVA), one of New York's most prominent art and design colleges, requested that Spiegelman join its staff as a professor that year, a position he held until 1987. Once at SVA, he not only had the chance to instruct students but to scout out new artistic talent.

## RAW Deal

In the 1980s, in keeping with Spiegelman's more academic and intellectual comics pursuits, he and Françoise Mouly cofounded a new, groundbreaking comics magazine. They named it *RAW*, and during the coming decade, it would become the premier place for up-and-coming comic artists to showcase their talents. *RAW* also gave Spiegelman the chance to flex his muscles as an editor in a way he had not previously enjoyed. Like most small-press books, *RAW* started out with a minimal circulation, but it was tremendously satisfying from a creative standpoint for both Spiegelman and his new wife. *RAW* represented a continuation of the work he had started with Bill Griffith in *Arcade*. Publishing a magazine required great effort, but as Spiegelman recalled in a 1991 interview in the *St. Louis Post-Dispatch*:

> [Arcade] was sort of a life-raft for lots of people involved in underground comix when that whole movement seemed to be

sinking. It lasted a couple of years and was a tremendous headache and a lot of work, and when it ended, I swore I'd never be involved with a magazine again. Then I moved to New York and met Françoise Mouly, and she wanted to do a magazine and I said, "Sure!" despite having sworn never to do it again.

When *RAW* debuted, it was not intended to be the first issue of an ongoing comic magazine, just a single print run. However, all 4,500 copies sold out, and it was obvious that the 1980s would find an audience that was curious about a variety of comics. Friends who were interested in both contributing to and reading more of *RAW* pushed Spiegelman and Mouly to continue producing the magazine. Soon, a second issue appeared in 1980. After that, they released one large-format issue annually until 1986.

*RAW* contained a mix of comic artists that included holdouts from the 1960s, including Robert Crumb; European artists whose work had never appeared in the United States; and old works from comic-strip legends that were reprinted. Spiegelman and Mouly also took the opportunity to act as first-rate talent scouts, keeping their eyes open for up-and-coming artists all over the country. Spiegelman gave rising young talents like Gary Panter, Charles Burns, Richard Sala, Kaz, Drew Friedman, Julie Doucet, and numerous others a place in the popular magazine, which soon led to bigger opportunities. Burns became a hugely successful illustrator and album-cover artist who had an MTV show based on

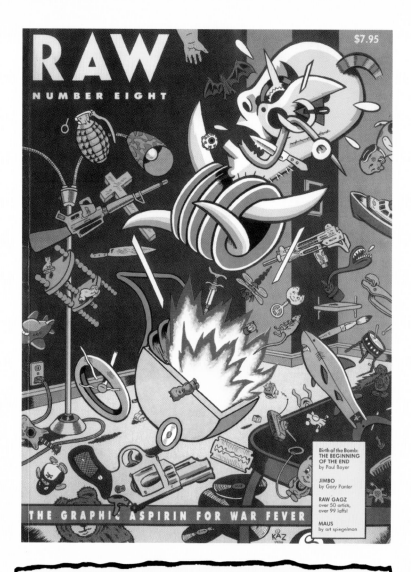

Although Spiegelman remembers the oversized, attention-grabbing anthologies of *RAW* ("The Graphix Magazine for Damned Intellectuals") as a headache to produce, he and his wife, Françoise Mouly, lovingly began the project in 1980 as a forum where underground comic artists could publish their wares. While the last oversized issue was completed in 1986, Penguin Publishing assumed the printing and distribution of a newer, book-sized *RAW* a few years later, also under the supervision of Spiegelman and Mouly. This cover of *RAW*, issue eight, was drawn by Kaz and printed in 1987. When *RAW* started in 1980, its print run was only about 4,500 copies; in 1991, the anthology was selling more than 40,000 copies per issue.

his character, Dog Boy. Panter, whose Jimbo character was a regular feature in *RAW*, designed the sets and characters for Paul Reubens's television show, *Pee Wee's Playhouse*. And Friedman became one of the premier illustrators in the magazine industry.

Those first issues of *RAW* were not only a place for other contributing artists to show their work, but a forum for Spiegelman himself to premier what would become his signature piece, the long-form comic *Maus*. Spiegelman's *Maus* appeared as inserts in the first six issues before being collected and republished in book form in 1986. It was the same year that the last large-format issue of *RAW* was printed. Spiegelman and Mouly believed that the magazine had lost its freshness. They wanted to avoid publishing work they felt was too predictable, so they took some time off. When *RAW* returned in 1989, it did so in a smaller format. And it now had the support of a major publisher, Penguin Publishing.

Penguin released *RAW* annually, boosting its overall circulation. By 1991, when the third issue under Penguin was released, its circulation had grown to about 40,000 copies. While some fans of the magazine felt that the smaller, book-sized issues were an unusual format for *RAW*, it made sense to Spiegelman. As he explained in the *St. Louis Post-Dispatch*, "The original *RAW* concentrated on art, and the large format presented that in a dramatic fashion. The current version is more a literary magazine." The new *RAW* had grown up with the intention of including longer pieces from the artists, with less graphic flash.

# From the Cabbage Patch to the Garbage Pail

The 1980s not only contained some of Spiegelman's most satisfying creative work, but he struck commercial gold in an entirely different, and unlikely, pursuit: lampooning a popular children's toy by designing a set of trading cards. In the early 1980s, Cabbage Patch Kids were one of the most popular toys for children. The dolls were cloth and rubber babies with large, innocent eyes and chubby faces. When you purchased a Cabbage Patch doll, it came complete with special "adoption papers," giving it an added dose of individuality with its own name and place of origin. The dolls were popular with both boys and girls, and soon, around holiday time, parents rushed to local toy stores around the country to grab—and sometimes fight—to get a hold of the next big thing.

Meanwhile, Spiegelman was doing creative consulting and artwork for Topps, a chewing gum company. He had worked for Topps from time to time since the mid-1960s. Topps also made much of its money manufacturing trading cards that accompanied each piece of its gum. Topps produces baseball cards and Bazooka Joe—nearly any character that translated well to trading cards. And while working for Topps, Spiegelman became involved in the creation of its Wacky Packages, visual parodies of well-known advertising designs and packaging.

For this idea, Spiegelman found inspiration in the recent and massive Cabbage Patch Kids phenomenon.

NERVOUS REX

He and three other partners—Mark Newgarden, John Pound, and Jay Lynch—proposed their idea, and Topps began putting out a new series of trading cards called the Garbage Pail Kids. The new characters were the direct result of all of Spiegelman's exposure to *Mad* magazine, especially the work of Harvey Kurtzman. While *Mad* influenced almost everything Spiegelman had done, his Garbage Pail Kids were perhaps the most direct homage to *Mad* ever.

Spiegelman's Garbage Pail Kids had a slight resemblance to the Cabbage Patch Kids, in that they were wide-eyed, chubby infants, but the paintings on Spiegelman's trading cards could not be called cute or innocent in any way. They were, in fact, obnoxious and disgusting versions of the popular dolls. The kids also had silly names that reflected their gross depiction such as "Weird Wendell," who had clothes under his skin; "Bony Joanie," an adorable, pig-tailed skeleton; and "Adam Bomb," who sported an exploding mushroom cloud on his head. Another popular favorite was "New Wave Dave," who doubled as a punk with a Mohawk hairstyle.

The kids, whom Spiegelman and Topps had intended to issue to make fun of the Cabbage Patch phenomenon, ended up becoming just as popular as the actual dolls. While the first series sold poorly, they soon became a huge success. Kids went berserk for the hilarious, grotesque cards just like earlier generations of the 1950s had gone crazy for *Mad*. Topps put out several series of the cards, each one more popular than the next. Although kids loved them, parents and teachers took one look at the grinning skeletons, acne-riddled freaks, and snotty, mucus-covered infants of the Garbage Pail Kids and said, "No way."

Public school systems all over the United States banned the Garbage Pail Kids from their classrooms, and many parents took them away from their kids. While some artists would have been upset that their work was being banned, Spiegelman loved it. As a former member of the underground comix scene, he still enjoyed getting a reaction from institutions like schools and the government. Spiegelman was paid what he considered to be the highest compliment when a state official from West Virginia explained on television why he was trying to get the Garbage Pail Kids outlawed in his state—he compared them to the older *Mad* magazines

While the Garbage Pail Kids eventually fizzled out after having sold millions of cards (and leading to the creation of a full-length feature film), the experience of having designed them remained a positive one for Spiegelman. He believed that it was important to expose children to the cards, saying in the *St. Louis Post-Dispatch*, "It [taught] kids to 'just say no.' Just say no to received ideas; to things that are being peddled to them that they don't have to think about." Many of the goals he tried to achieve with the underground comix, and that he had begun with *RAW*, were accomplished on a huge scale with the creation of the Garbage Pail Kids. It became the greatest exposure his work had received.

## The New Underground

The late 1980s saw a new underground developing in the comics industry. Publishers like Dark Horse, Kitchen Sink, and Fantagraphics were issuing work outside of the mainstream of DC and Marvel. DC, once the model of comic conservatism, had launched a successful imprint of adult-oriented comics called *Vertigo*. The imprint showcased a largely English

Spiegelman and Mouly review drawings for an upcoming book in this photograph taken in 1987. The pair's winning combination of artistic talent (Mouly is art director for *New Yorker* magazine) and spousal support has resulted in many cutting-edge projects including *RAW* and *Little Lit: Folklore & Fairytale Funnies*, an anthology of comic narratives for children.

group of writers and artists who were interested in crafting serious works of fiction out of comics. The European concept of comics as genuine and important art was slowly influencing the American mainstream comic scene. Creators like Alan Moore and Neil Gaiman started working on American titles and brought a whole new perspective to the idea of traditional heroes and villains.

Other voices arose, too, as comics like *Love and Rockets*, about life in Latino sections of Los Angeles, were published and successfully received. Creators like Daniel Clowes and Peter Bagge, who followed in the tradition of the underground comix scene of the 1960s, released their first works. Clowes, in particular, would later find great success, even receiving an Oscar nomination for his screenplay *Ghost World*. The dark world of Charles Burns existed alongside the immigrant urban anxiety of French Canadian Julie Doucet, while Kaz, Richard Sala, and the highly acclaimed Chris Ware all continued releasing popular comics. Joe Sacco wrote hard-nosed journalistic comics that brought detailed, gutsy, and political war reporting onto the comics page for the first time. It seemed as though women and men of every background were producing a variety of comics for a diverse readership. By 1990, comics were more varied than they had been since the late 1960s, and it would not be a stretch to say that Spiegelman was largely responsible for the momentum.

Spiegelman, who had never given up on the idea that comics could reach a wider audience, was heralded as a leader. His and Mouly's *RAW* magazine had given voices to many comic artists and innovators who had been previously unknown. The new cartoonists that blossomed in the late 1980s represented a *RAW* generation. As Chuck Stephens wrote in the *San Francisco Bay Guardian* in 2000, "the irregularly published *RAW* was the epicenter of post-everything comic book culture. Post-superhero, post-pornographic, post Museum-of-Modern-Art."

*RAW*'s impact had a great influence on American pop culture. When someone picked up a copy of Iggy Pop's album *Brick by Brick*, he or she was looking at Charles Burns's work. When parents and kids watched *Pee Wee's Playhouse*, they saw Gary Panter's creations. Daniel Clowes's *Ghost World* made comics larger than life on the big screen. Spiegelman had used *RAW* to bring comic culture to the masses, and it worked marvelously. But what *RAW* would end up being best remembered for was Spiegelman's own work of autobiographical fiction, *Maus*.

# CHAPTER 4

# MAUS I AND THE HOLOCAUST

Spiegelman's parents, Anja and Vladek, were just two of the few survivors of the Holocaust. The Holocaust is a blanket term that describes the death of approximately 6 million (mostly) Jewish men, women, and children at the hands of Nazi officials. Nazi Germany, led by *führer* (leader) Adolf Hitler, aimed to eliminate Jewish people from all lands controlled by Germany. To do so, the Nazis rounded up Jews and sent them to concentration camps, where horrible conditions and certain death awaited most of them. Many of these camps served as death camps, where those who couldn't work were shot or gassed, then burned in crematoriums.

Since World War I (1914–1918), Germany's economy had been in shambles. The German government, blamed for starting the war, was forced by the victorious Allied nations to pay huge war debts to the countries they had wronged. Citizens were looking for a scapegoat for Germany's troubles, and many turned their sights to the Jews. As an ethnic minority, German Jews found themselves surrounded by hatred and jealousy from many of their "pure" German neighbors. Hitler, a failed art student from Austria, had been using Jewish hatred, or anti-Semitism, to empower himself. As early as 1919, Hitler wrote about the Jews, describing them as a race rather than a religious group. He called them "sub-human" and blamed them for all of Germany's economic problems. Many German people, desperate to ease their suffering and lay blame, believed Hitler's dogmatic ideas. Soon, many Germans saw Hitler as the man to turn the economy around and elected him to office. When he rose to power in 1933, Hitler took the first steps toward what would eventually be known as the Holocaust. Although Hitler was supported by the Germans during his rise to power, they knew nothing of his plan to eventually exterminate the Jewish people.

Once in power in 1933, Hitler and the Nazis began dismantling the Jewish community within their own borders, taking away their businesses, homes, and freedoms. In addition to the Jews, the Nazis persecuted Gypsies (or *Roma*), homosexuals, Jehovah's Witnesses, and Germans with mental or physical deformities. Not satisfied with control over Germany, the Nazis set out to expand Germany's borders by conquering all of Europe. The larger Nazi goal was to conquer the whole world. World War II began when

Die Socialdemocratie

im „Spiegel der Wahrheit", dargestellt vom „Kikeriki".

This caricature of a Jewish man, printed in the 1920s anti-Semitic Viennese magazine *Kikeriki*, is but one example of how Jews were often portrayed as stereotypes. Its text reads, "Social Democracy in the 'mirror of truth' ad portrayed by Kikeriki." The man is holding a money bag, inside his jacket is an envelope marked "collections," and on the mirror are the words "the noble race."

Germany invaded Poland, where the Spiegelman family had lived.

The Spiegelmans' experience during the Holocaust was horrific. Vladek and Anja Spiegelman suffered unbelievably, and the experience would haunt them throughout their lives, perhaps later contributing to Anja's suicide in 1968. Art Spiegelman had always injected the personal, controversial, and political into his comic work, and at the start of the 1980s, he decided to tell his family's story. The work, which would eventually become the graphic novel *Maus*, originally appeared in six serialized chapters in *RAW* magazine between 1980 and 1986. In the end, *Maus* became Spiegelman's greatest work, and an example of how comics could become something greater than merely entertainment.

## Not So Funny Aminals

The first glimpse of the drawings that would become *Maus* appeared as a three-page story in a 1972 comic called *Funny Aminals* (misspelling intentional). For *Maus*, Spiegelman used one of comics' most familiar stylistic approaches. For decades, alongside super-heroes, "funny animal" comics were some of the biggest sellers. Disney artist Carl Barks's Donald Duck had long been a staple of the comics world. Many of the artists in the underground comix movement had grown up reading animal comics, and creators such as Robert Crumb and Bill Griffith used familiar types of animal characters in very different, and increasingly adult, ways. Spiegelman, being deeply involved in the underground scene, saw an opportunity with *Maus* to turn the notion of funny animals on its ear. In truth, he had confessed to seeing "something sober" in Barks's Donald Duck. The story presented in *Maus* is Vladek Spiegelman's story, but on the surface, it's also the story of a family of mice and the cats that destroy them.

In Nazi Germany, Jewish people had been reduced and simplified into crude, one-dimensional stereotypes.

Nazi authorities had been successful at portraying the Jewish people as inhuman misers. Hitler and the Nazis knew that it would be easier for people to hurt and mistreat the Jews if they appeared not as people, but as "types." While writing *Maus*, Spiegelman saw the opportunity to use the underground comix fixation with animals as a clever tool to show how the different ethnic groups viewed each other.

To that end, the Spiegelman family and other Jews were presented as mice. The Poles were pigs, the Germans cats, and the Americans dogs. The deadly serious story was presented in a way that comics' fans could recognize, but with a totally different effect.

When *Maus* was published later, the work was divided into two major parts. *Part One: My Father Bleeds History* comprised the individual chapters that appeared in *RAW* between 1980 and 1986. *Part Two: And Here My Troubles Began* appeared later, in 1991. This was a publishing schedule very different from the monthly comics that Spiegelman and others his age were accustomed to seeing. *Maus I* wasn't issued in one collected volume until it was completed. In fact, Vladek Spiegelman never lived to see his full life story in print. He died in 1982.

## The Survivor

After the 1972 story in *Funny Aminals*, Spiegelman began a series of interviews with his father that he eventually used in the creation of *Maus*, which was shaped by Vladek's memories, but partially took place in the present day. Art Spiegelman was not only the writer and artist of the story, but also a character in it. *Maus* is told to the reader by Spiegelman's pen, but at the same time, ideas reflected in the piece are told to the artist by his father. Even after Spiegelman's father died, the work included the sequences of their conversations. Spiegelman himself wondered if it was his way of maintaining a relationship with his father. He said in the *St. Louis Post-Dispatch*, "In many ways I have a better relationship with him now than I did when he was alive."

By including himself in the story, Spiegelman made *Maus* something much more personal than earlier readers were accustomed to seeing. Readers of *Maus* don't only see the hardships that Vladek and his family endured in Poland during World War II, they see the difficulties that Spiegelman had to endure in his strained relationship with his father. The extra personal layer of the story gave *Maus* a depth that comics, even autobiographical stories, had lacked up until that time.

*Maus I: My Father Bleeds History* did not report about life in the concentration camps. It begins in Czestochowa, Poland, where Vladek Spiegelman worked in textile sales. *Maus* starts in an upbeat tone, covering Vladek and Anja's courtship, their marriage, and the birth of their first child, Richieu. Unfortunately, their happiness is short-lived. The beginning of their lives together coincided with Hitler's aggression against Poland, and Vladek was drafted into the Polish army to defend its borders against the mighty Germans. When

Before the first volume of *Maus: My Father Bleeds History* was published by Pantheon in 1986, individual chapters of the book debuted in *RAW*, as separate tiny pull-out comics between 1980 and 1986, as shown on this page. The *Maus* "comic within a comic" format was a hit, and it encouraged sales of *RAW*, as readers were eager to follow the engaging story from issue to issue. This chapter of *Maus* originally appeared in *RAW*, number 8, in 1986.

the fighting began in the fall of 1939, Vladek found himself forced to kill a German soldier. The Poles were quickly defeated, and the nightmare that was the German occupation of Poland began.

## Prisoner of War

When Germany invaded Poland, Vladek Spiegelman was captured and brought to a camp as a prisoner of war. At the camp, Jewish soldiers were separated from the other prisoners. They were forced to perform hard manual labor and were barely fed. When an opportunity to work in a prison camp with better conditions presented itself, Vladek eagerly took it. Life in the new camp was an improvement, with a bed and four walls, but it was still prison, and Vladek remained separated from his family.

Vladek's future in the prison camp was uncertain. One night, he had a dream in which his dead grandfather told him that he would be freed in three months. Although it was only a dream, it gave Vladek hope. Sure enough, several months later a battery of German troops arrived at the work camp. Vladek signed papers, told the German soldiers his destination of Sosnowiec, and was put on a train. As far as he knew, he was free. However, in Hitler's Europe, things were more complicated.

When Germany first invaded Poland, the country was divided into two parts: the Reich and the Protectorate. The Reich, which contained Sosnowiec, was annexed to Germany. The Protectorate was under German control, but still considered Poland. After having traveled many miles on the train, it became clear to Vladek that it was not stopping in Sosnowiec. About 300 miles (483 kilometers) from where he was supposed to be released, Vladek and the other Jewish prisoners of war (POWs) were taken off of the trains and brought to another work camp in the Reich. They didn't know what to expect and were soon given bad news by Jewish officials. The group of 600 people who had come before them had been killed.

As citizens of the Reich, Vladek's group was not covered by international POW laws, according to the Nazis. A Jew in the Reich had no protection against inhumane treatment. Jews could be shot in the street if German officials so desired. Realizing that he would be killed if he stayed, Vladek worked on an escape plan. With the help of local Jewish officials, Vladek pretended to be the cousin of a local friend who came and picked him up from the camp, saving his life for the time being. The next problem, though, was that of sneaking over the Protectorate's borders into the Reich to return to Sosnowiec and back to his family.

In German-occupied territories, people needed official documents to travel over borders. Vladek, as a former POW, had no papers. He decided to masquerade as a non-Jewish Pole, hoping that the train conductor would be sympathetic and allow him aboard. While in reality Vladek needed nothing to hide his Jewish heritage, in *Maus* Spiegelman depicts Vladek wearing a pig mask, appearing to be disguised as a Pole. The plan worked, and Vladek was finally reunited with his family. It was his first daring escape, but it would not be his last.

## No Place Like Home

Returning to his homeland, Vladek Spiegelman found a very different Poland under the German occupation. As the Nazi grip tightened, Polish Jews found their liberties increasingly violated. Vladek first searched for his parents. His father, a devoutly religious man, had been beaten and mocked in the streets along with a group of fellow Jews. Their distinctive beards, a part of their culture, had been shaved off. Also, his father's seltzer factory had been confiscated and given to an Aryan (a name used in Nazi Germany for "pure" white Germans) manager. Vladek's mother had fallen ill and would be dead from cancer within a few months.

When Vladek returned to his wife, child, and in-laws (the Zylberbergs), he found the situation was equally bad for them. His father-in-law's household, while still fairly luxurious, was now holding a dozen people, including Anja's grandparents, both in their nineties. The family was better off than many, but still had trouble obtaining enough food. Polish Jews were given food coupons, which provided meager rations but kept many of them alive. However, their businesses, like Vladek's textile factory, had been taken over by German managers. The family had no way of making a living and no income. The Nazis were also imposing harsh, unjust laws on Polish people in general. If anyone broke a Nazi law, he or she would be carted off to a work camp.

The Spiegelmans lived this way in the Zylberberg home for more than a year, in relative comfort. Vladek and the other men in the family found work through other Jewish friends. Vladek collected some money he was owed before the war broke out, and he was able to find work in a tin shop that did work for Nazi officials. The job kept him safe as it provided him with a priority work card—the Nazis were less likely to harass a Jew who worked for them.

As 1940 wore on, the family felt the grip of Nazi persecution tighten. Jews were being rounded up and taken away in the streets without explanation, and Nazis were seizing furniture and other valuable goods from Jewish homes. Vladek barely escaped capture on several occasions, and he started to believe that his son Richieu would be better off hiding with another family. Anja would not hear of it, however, and Richieu remained with them.

## Relocation

Eventually, the Nazis ordered the Spiegelman and Zylberberg families, along with all other Jewish families in Sosnowiec, to abandon their homes. They were forced to move to another section of town. It wasn't quite a ghetto, but it resembled one. The Spiegelmans were initially able to move around with some freedom, but they were expected back in their area by nightfall. They had now lost much of what they once had, for no reason other than their religion. Their new home was a small three-room apartment. All twelve of them, including the elderly, squeezed into it.

It was increasingly difficult for relocated Jews to make an honest living, and a thriving black market began in the Jewish quarter. Vladek Spiegelman readily took part in it. One day, four of his new business associates were captured by soldiers and hanged. Their dead bodies were left outside in plain view for a full week. The Nazi message was clear: "Do business our way, or never do business again."

## The First Stirrings of Auschwitz

In the second part of *Maus*, *And Here My Troubles Began*, Spiegelman wrote about life under brutal conditions in the concentration camps. Initially, the relocated Jews did not know about such death factories, but rumors of their existence and of what transpired there were becoming known.

In the early Nazi years, the regime debated about what to do with the Jews. They did not want them in their country and simply considered kicking them out. Deportation was contemplated for a long time, but Nazi officials ultimately decided that it was impractical. The Nazis' "Final Solution" to the Jewish question was to exterminate them. Ultimately, the Nazis had death camps built, complete with gas chambers and crematoriums. The Nazis planned to kill some Jews outright and work others to death.

This panel originally appeared in chapter four of *Maus I: My Father Bleeds History*. It depicts the murder of four Jews in Poland who had been trading goods on the black market without coupons (or, in other words, without the approval of the Nazi government). The action represents a turning point in the narrative of the story, for Spiegelman's father now understood that the Nazis crossed over from merely oppressing Jews to eliminating them.

Six concentration camps were constructed, all in German-occupied Poland, and were operational by 1942. Auschwitz, perhaps the most notorious, and the camp that eventually housed the Spiegelmans, actually comprised three sections: Auschwitz, Birkenau, and Buna-Monowitz. Birkenau was the section of the camp that served as the extermination center.

The death camps were operated like a business with maximum efficiency. Prisoners were transported to the camps in trains, sometimes in cattle cars. After disembarking, Jews immediately faced the *selektion* process. This meant that prisoners were separated into two groups. In one line were placed pregnant women, young children, the sick, the handicapped, and the elderly. Such prisoners were immediately sent to the gas chamber to die. Prisoners in the second line were those deemed fit to work. They were then forced to live in filthy conditions, given little food, and made to work until they could work no more. Camps like this were partially funded by German corporations, including IG Farben, which benefited from the slave labor and was also responsible for creating Zyklon B (a type of poisonous gas), which was used to kill those people sent to the gas chambers. The prisoners were worked to death, and if ever one became too sick to work, he or she was sent to the gas chamber and killed.

To the relocated Jews who were forced to work in Sosnowiec's Jewish quarter and in similar sections in other cities, the existence of such death camps was too horrible to comprehend. To many, it seemed like a terrible rumor. Some of the first people taken away to the camps were elderly, as they could not work as long or as hard as younger people could.

In Poland, the Zylberbergs, Spiegelmans, and other Jewish families received notice that any Jew over seventy years of age was to be transported to an elderly convalescent home in Czechoslovakia on May 10, 1942. Since Anja's grandparents were older than seventy, this notice applied to them. Although they didn't know anything about the gas chambers at Auschwitz-Birkenau, they were still afraid. They feared never seeing their families again.

Not knowing what would become of the grandparents, the family built a secret hiding place for them in a shed out in the yard. Secret hiding places such as this would become common throughout German-occupied Poland as families struggled to remain together. The family had to relinquish Anja's grandparents to the authorities when officials threatened to take its youngest members instead. The Zylberbergs believed the grandparents were going to a convalescent home, but the Nazis had lied. The grandparents were sent to Auschwitz-Birkenau, where they died in a gas chamber.

Anja's grandparents were the first family members to disappear. As the war and occupation in Poland wore on, the Spiegelmans and Zylberbergs saw their ranks thin out in heartbreaking ways. Shortly after the grandparents were removed, Nazi officials announced that everyone in the Jewish quarter of Sosnowiec would have to register at a stadium. By then, word of the death camps had spread, and people were consumed with fear of what might occur at the registration.

Vladek's father, who had been living with his daughter and her children, did not know if he should go to the stadium. Like many other citizens, he was afraid that it would be just another Nazi excuse to round up the Jews. At the same time, people were afraid of the repercussions they might face if they stayed away. Without the registration papers that might be issued at the stadium, there would be nothing to stop the Nazis from arresting them. In the end, both families went to the registration.

Vladek and the rest of Anja's family were spared. However, Vladek's sister, Fela, and her four children were separated from the group. Rather than leave his only daughter and grandchildren to face the unknown alone, Vladek's father, who had been spared, climbed a fence over to the rejected group. Vladek never saw his sister or father again. They, like so many other Jews, were either killed or relocated to another ghetto.

As Vladek relates the story of his family's struggle to his son in *Maus*, he is presented as a distracted person— one preoccupied by things going on in his life in the present. Vladek is concerned about his relationship with his new wife, his son's shabby jacket, the price of phone cords, and other small matters. But this is only an indication of how much the events of World War II deeply affected him.

For Vladek, retelling the story of his last meeting with his father was too much to endure, so he asked Spiegelman if they could stop for the day. Throughout *Maus*, Spiegelman breaks up the story of the past with pieces of his interview with his father in the present. The same young man who had everything taken away from him during World War II is, in the present, a normal old man in a home in Queens, New York. He has small, petty arguments with his second wife; he complains about the price of tape recorders; and he is grumpy and impatient. At times, he seems like a completely different person.

Although Anja had died by the time Spiegelman wrote *Maus*, his mother also played a large role in its

In these panels, Spiegelman recounts the misery surrounding the first selection of men, women, and children who would eventually end up in the concentration camps in Auschwitz. Although Polish Jews were told by the Nazis that they should show up for an inspection of their documents by Nazi officials, people were instead segregated according to their age, health, prior work experience, and the size of their family.

process. While working through his memories of the Holocaust, Vladek is forced to examine the memory of Anja and her suicide. At one point in *Maus*, finding a copy of his son's comic that recounts Anja's suicide, "Prisoner on the Hell Planet," disturbs Vladek. Adding another level of dimension to *Maus*, Spiegelman reprinted the entire "Hell Planet" comic in *Maus* without guiding the reader in what to think about the older work or its disturbing contents. Spiegelman brings his mother's suicide into the middle of this Holocaust story—a Holocaust she has also lived through. Who knows what kind of horror followed Anja from 1940s Poland all the way to New York? Escaping the death camps with her life, but without her son Richieu, may not have been enough in the end.

# CHAPTER 5

# THE DEATH CAMPS AND MAUS II

In *Maus*, Spiegelman relived his parents' losses during the war. Not only did Vladek's father and sister die, but so did Spiegelman's brother, Richieu. Vladek and Anja knew a man of influence in another town in Poland. They were convinced that the worst was yet to come, so they decided to send Richieu away with Vladek's brother-in-law Wolfe, and his wife, Tosha. The couple took the child and escaped to Zawiercie, where the local head of the Jewish council wielded some influence. Vladek was willing to do almost anything to spare his son from Auschwitz-Birkenau, even if it meant not seeing him until the war was over.

However, a few months after Richieu relocated, the Nazis closed the Zawiercie ghetto. Terrifying rumors spread about Nazis torturing and killing children in other ghettos. It was now clear that their eventual destination would be the feared death camps. Tosha could not stand the thought of going to Auschwitz and could not allow the other children to be taken away. To avoid the inevitable, she poisoned herself and all of the children in her care, including Richieu. Spiegelman would never meet his brother.

## Hiding in the Walls

Spiegelman's metaphorical depiction of Jews as mice in *Maus* worked well for various reasons. Among them was the fact that during the occupation, many Jews were forced to create secret holes behind walls and above ceilings to avoid being discovered by the Nazis. Spiegelman's father described the elaborate hiding places constructed by the Jews that truly resembled nothing more than mouse holes. In Srodula, Poland, where the Zylberbergs and Spiegelmans were relocated in 1943, they were able to build a secret hiding place under a coal bin in the kitchen. It involved a tunnel to the basement and a false wall. Conditions in these temporary bunkers were cramped, unsanitary, and disgusting, and Vladek described them explicitly.

The family relocated yet again to a different house and had to create another hiding place. This secret place was built in the attic, where they were concealed by a false wall. It had an entrance that was hidden by a chandelier in the ceiling. The family stayed in the attic at all times except to gather food. The conditions were even more cramped, and no one knew how long they could

Spiegelman's father, Vladek, explains to Spiegelman the hiding place that he created in Srodula for his family and the Zylberbergs. Although the Nazis were feverishly searching for any remaining Jews in the village, the families managed to survive on rations there for several days before they could escape to another homemade bunker.

hold out up there. This worked for a while, but at the end of July in 1943, the family left the Srodula ghetto as well. A Jewish informant discovered them and turned them in to the Nazis. They were quickly arrested and taken to another part of the ghetto that was enclosed in barbed wire.

From there, it was only a matter of time before they would be taken away to Auschwitz. One day, while waiting for the transport van, Vladek spotted his cousin Jakov in a nearby courtyard. He offered to pay Jakov to help him sneak his family out of the ghetto, and Jakov agreed. The next day, a man named Haskel, a chief of the Jewish police, and Jakov helped sneak Vladek, Anja, and Vladek's nephew Lolek out. However, nothing could be done to save Anja's parents. They were too old to make it past the guards—the Nazis had already exterminated most of the older Jews. They gave the guard some of the family's jewels, and he took them, but the risk was too great. Anja's parents were taken away to Auschwitz when the next van came; they were gassed shortly after their arrival.

Many readers of *Maus* find it heart-wrenching when they realize that these events actually happened and that Vladek was forced to watch his family suffer.

In this panel from *Maus: My Father Bleeds History*, Vladek and Anja were heading for a new hiding place in Sosnowiec. High above the street where they walked, a Polish woman recognized Anja Spiegelman and called out, "There's a Jewess in the courtyard!" Although the Spiegelmans had survived the first rounds of extermination, they were still at risk for being discovered as Jews and sent to the concentration camps in Auschwitz.

Many stories about the Holocaust exist, and among those many memoirs *Maus* stands out as being unique—reading it is like reliving Spiegelman's conversations with his father. It's rare that readers get to see the author's reaction to something at the same time they are reading it. Spiegelman seems to be hearing about the final fate of many relatives at the same time that we, as readers, are. And it's this very interview with his father that we are both watching unfold.

Along with the devastating account of the Holocaust, Spiegelman continuously adds details about his father's present life. As Vladek recounts the events at Srodula, the reader realizes that Vladek is very ill, as his son finds it necessary to give him a pill for his heart while they are out walking. In reality, Vladek died in 1982, long before *Maus* was completed, and never got to see his story fully documented.

## The Coming Storm

By the end of 1943, the Spiegelmans were staying with Vladek's cousin Haskel and his two brothers in relative comfort in Srodula. Haskel was well connected in the ghetto, and as a member of the Jewish police, he provided some protection to the Spiegelmans. He even played cards with the Nazi guards, letting them win so they would like him. Haskel and his brothers ran a shoe shop, and when they heard rumors of the pending closure of the Srodula ghetto, one of Haskel's brothers made plans to build a tunnel under a pile of shoes that led to a large bunker. The Spiegelmans went with Haskel to the bunker, but Lolek, Vladek's fifteen-year-old-nephew, did not. He was tired of hiding. Lolek was taken away to Auschwitz around the same time that Anja found out that her son Richieu had been poisoned. Besides Vladek, she had no family left at all.

When Anja heard of Richieu's death, she didn't want to live anymore. She begged Vladek to let her die. Anja pulled through at the time, but the desire to end her life never truly disappeared.

## The Waiting Game

When the Nazis closed Srodula, the Spiegelmans sought safety in the bunker near the shoe shop. Space was tight as twelve people crammed into the tiny shelter. No one had any food, and Vladek and Anja chewed on wood to help them forget their constant hunger. They waited until the guards were gone, then came out to find the ghetto completely empty. With the Nazis gone, they were free for the moment.

Vladek managed to save many of the valuable objects that he had in his possession in the Srodula ghetto and took them to the United States after the war. Some of these heirlooms even surfaced during Spiegelman's interview with his father. Vladek had hidden them in a chimney in Srodula and went back for them when he was released from the camps in 1945. The extreme measures he took to preserve a few jewels and a cigarette case remained a testament to his struggle to escape World War II with even the smallest shred of his former life intact.

Despite underlining his father's heroic survival during such harsh wartime conditions, Spiegelman refused to hide his father's flaws in *Maus*. Spiegelman allows his own anger toward his father to surface when he discovers that Vladek discarded his mother's old diaries after the war. He also keeps in a bit when his father exhibits his own racial prejudice in *Maus II*. Although *Maus* is a comic featuring talking animals, the idea of journalistic integrity in the story was very important to Spiegelman. As such, he approached the discussions with his father just like any other writer would an important interview. However, part of the downside of this, as shown in the finished *Maus*, was that his father was portrayed as merely a caricature while Spiegelman tried to show him in an objective and honest light as possible.

His quest for unsparing accuracy included his father's extreme frugal nature—a stereotype that anti-Semites have often unfairly attributed to Jews. Vladek Spiegelman had lived through the Great Depression, a time of economic hardship that probably contributed to his thrifty tendencies. In the end, we witness Spiegelman's struggle with the idea of furthering stereotypes right there on the page through a conversation with his stepmother. Spiegelman allows the reader to see his psychological process and his doubts about creating *Maus*—another fresh, provocative approach that gained *Maus* a great deal of praise.

## The Wanderers

After hiding out in the bunker until the Nazis were gone, Vladek and Anja were without a place to go. They were free, but had no safe home. They walked toward Sosnowiec, finding safe haven here and there with old friends. However, many people were willing to turn Jews over to the Nazis. For this part of the story in *Maus*, Spiegelman drew his parents wearing pig masks, showing that they were pretending to be non-Jewish Poles.

Vladek and Anja found a suitable hiding place in a basement of a woman Vladek met in the black market. The woman's husband worked in Germany and returned home only once every three months for about ten days. The Spiegelmans had many close calls, and Vladek and Anja were repeatedly forced to hide the fact that they were Jews. They had to stay in the basement when the woman's husband came home. Eventually, Vladek cooked up a plan to escape to Hungary. He had heard it was safe there, and he paid money to have himself and Anja smuggled out of Poland. Although it seemed like the best plan, it quickly backfired. After an hour on the train, they reached Bielsko, where Vladek once owned a factory. The Nazis came aboard and started a raid—there was no escape. Vladek and Anja Spiegelman's long run was over.

## The Camp

The Nazis marched the Jews though Bielsko, and Vladek saw many of his old haunts. As the Spiegelmans were

After years of running and hiding during World War II, Spiegelman's parents, Vladek and Anja, finally arrive by train in Auschwitz in 1944. Although they had managed to remain together through most of the tragedy, they were finally separated into different camps. At this point, they feared they would suffer the same fate as many Jews had before them: certain death by poisonous gas.

taken away, all their possessions were stolen. After a few days of captivity, they, along with about 100 others, were taken to Auschwitz.

By now, they were well aware of what happened at the camps. As far as Vladek and Anja knew, they were moments away from being put in a gas chamber, then burned in a crematorium. To make matters worse, they had been separated—the Nazis made male and female prisoners live in different areas. Vladek and Anja did not know if they would ever see each other again.

## And Here My Troubles Began

*Maus I* ends with Spiegelman's parents arriving at Auschwitz, each going to a separate camp. This part of the story ended in a 1986 issue of *RAW*. Afterward, it was collected and released as a book. The critical reaction was highly favorable. The *Washington Post* called it "[a] quiet triumph, moving and simple—impossible to describe accurately, and impossible to achieve in any medium but comics." *Newsweek* said, "*Maus* compels us to bear witness in a different way: The very artificiality of its surface makes it possible to understand the reality beneath." Spiegelman was also nominated for a National Book Critics' Circle Award.

But Spiegelman had more of his parents' story to tell. Issue 8 of *RAW*, published in 1986, contained the first chapter of *Maus II*. It was titled *And Here My Troubles Began*. This was the last large format-issue of *RAW*, and *Maus II* would not continue until 1991.

*Maus II* reveals Vladek and Anja's story after their arrival at Auschwitz, where they find themselves at the mercy of the Nazis. In *Maus II*, however, Spiegelman allows more of his own story into the comic. It begins in 1979, during the period when Spiegelman was first conducting interviews with his father and working on preliminary sketches for *Maus*. Whereas *Maus I*

The cover for the 1991 book release of *Maus: A Survivor's Tale, Part II: And Here My Troubles Began*. Beginning at the end of *Maus I*, when Spiegelman's parents, Vladek and Anja, were captured and transported to Auschwitz, *Maus II* details their lives in the concentration camp until their release at the end of the war alongside tales of Spiegelman's own contemporary life in New York City.

features touches of Spiegelman's creative process through interviews with Vladek, *Maus II* spends more time on Spiegelman's present circumstances.

Thus, the story of *Maus II* takes place not only in 1944, but also in 1979, as Spiegelman and his wife, Françoise, take care of Vladek, whose second wife has left him. In fact, Françoise, who was barely pictured in the first *Maus*, appears frequently in *Maus II*. Spiegelman's character is even shown having a discussion with Françoise about how he plans to picture her in the story. Since she's French, Spiegelman isn't sure that he should depict her as a mouse. *Maus II* is as much a story about the Holocaust as it is one about the difficulties of creating the story itself.

Spiegelman shifts the time frame throughout *Maus II*. He begins chapter two, "Auschwitz (Time Flies)," with a description of his own state of mind at the time he began the comic in 1987. He writes about his father's death in 1982 and about the success of *Maus I*. Spiegelman mulls over the film offers he has received and the critical praise generated by his work. He also worries about the upcoming birth of his daughter, Nadja. Spiegelman fearlessly allows the reader into his own mind as he draws panels of himself visiting his psychotherapist, who is also a Holocaust survivor.

With his therapist's help, Spiegelman tries to get to the root of his depression at a time when his life couldn't be better. Are his depressed feelings an extension of his father's guilt for having survived after his wife chose to end her life? Is he feeling the same guilt his father felt after surviving in conditions that were far better than his own parents faced? Is he despondent about his deceased brother who never had a chance to grow up? By combining the events of the past with the influence they have on the present, Spiegelman broke boundaries in *Maus II* and further deepened his story and the story of his parents' ordeal.

## The Prisoner

In *Maus II*, Spiegelman retraces Vladek's attempt to adjust to the harsh conditions at Auschwitz. Upon his arrival, he and a friend named Mandlebaum were stripped of their clothes and shoes. They were forced to run in the snow to receive their new camp uniforms, which didn't fit. The wooden shoes they received were also the wrong size. They were fed meager rations and frequently abused. They were even branded with numerical tattoos. Still, Vladek managed to persevere.

When one of the Kapos (Polish bosses within the camp who helped the Nazis run things) needed someone to help him learn English, Vladek volunteered. While Vladek was afraid of what the job might entail, it turned out to be good decision. The Kapo had access to things that the other prisoners did not, like more-nourishing food, and he shared it with Vladek. He also helped Vladek avoid being killed or chosen for hard labor. Vladek eventually learned that he was the sole survivor of the group of men who had arrived at Auschwitz with him.

Although living with the Kapo kept Vladek safe for more than two months, he needed to begin working to

Vladek Spiegelman is pictured in these panels from *Maus II* showing the number tattooed on his arm by Nazi officials while he was imprisoned in Auschwitz. This photograph of Vladek (*bottom*) was taken while he was in Auschwitz. In the story, Vladek recounts the moment and how after his release, he mailed the image, along with a letter, to his wife to let her know he was still alive.

stay alive. He had previous blacksmithing skills and was able to find suitable work in the camp. It was another example of Vladek's resourcefulness. Although the situation was extremely difficult and people were dying all around him, Vladek continued to survive. A Polish priest told him that the number tattooed on his arm meant he would survive, and Vladek believed it.

## Anja's Auschwitz

While Vladek continued making the best of his situation, Anja was kept in the Birkenau section of Auschwitz, about 2 miles (3.2 km) away. Both physically and spiritually, Anja's health was not as good as Vladek's. She was forced to carry heavy barrels of soup and was beaten when it spilled. However, like Vladek, she was able to make a friend who had some influence. The friend, named Mancie, found out that Vladek was still alive and helped the two pass notes to each other.

Anja's placement at Birkenau was temporary. Birkenau was the section of Auschwitz where the gassings occurred. It was a terrifying place, but when Vladek had a chance to work on tin roofing there, he jumped at the chance to be closer to his wife. He needed to see her in person. Although he was shocked at how frail she had become, he was excited to find her alive. The brief visit strengthened the couple's hopes, and Vladek was able to return to see her several times. However, he was once caught speaking with Anja and was badly beaten afterward.

## Shoemaker Spiegelman

Vladek's boss at the tin shop was cruel, so Vladek secured other employment. He began working in a shoe shop repairing leather boots in a warm, dry room. Vladek was so good at his new job he was able to receive many favors for his excellent work. He even helped Anja by fixing her boots.

Vladek heard rumors that new barracks were being built, which would house some of the women near his own barracks. He was desperate to have Anja move to this new shelter so they could be near each other. Against the odds, he managed to secure 100 cigarettes and a bottle of vodka to offer as a bribe. Vladek had developed a habit of saving everything, even paper for notes. This trait remained with him in 1979, when the contemporary scenes of *Maus II* show him saving everything he possibly can. The bribe worked, and Anja was one of the prisoners moved to the new barracks. The couple was able to experience a little happiness together. They had to be careful, though, as Anja was almost caught when Vladek sent her a package.

Vladek's work situation soon changed, however, when the Nazis closed down the shoe shop. He was transferred to "black work," which consisted of hauling huge stones around outside all day. It was better than death, but not nearly as easy as repairing shoes.

## Selektion

From time to time, the Nazis would hold another *selektion* where workers who were too frail and weak were

SO I MARCHED WITH A FEW TIN-MEN OVER TO BIRKENAU. I CAME THE FIRST TIME IN SUMMER 1944

THOUSANDS - HUNDREDS OF THOUSANDS OF HUN-GARIANS WERE ARRIV-ING THERE AT THIS TIME.

In this panel from *Maus II*, Vladek Spiegelman is given an opportunity to leave Auschwitz and travel by train to the women's camp in Birkenau. Nazi officials often took prisoners from one camp to another to perform specific jobs, as in this case, where roofers were needed to repair shelters in Birkenau. At this point in the story, Vladek and his wife, Anja, had been separated for some time, and Vladek was hopeful that visiting Birkenau would give him the chance to find her.

taken away and killed. By the time he was doing black work, Vladek was thin and his health was declining. For the first time, he was unsure that he would make it through *selektion*. In yet another close call, he hid in the bathroom and was again spared.

Vladek spent between ten to twelve months at Auschwitz. In 1944, the Russian army, then part of the Allied forces, was moving in on German-occupied Poland. As the Russians edged closer, Vladek had the chance to work as a blacksmith again. But this time, the Nazis had a different reason for needing blacksmiths. Fearing that the Russian invaders would witness the atrocities at

Auschwitz, Nazi officials insisted that the extermination camps be deconstructed and all evidence destroyed. Vladek witnessed firsthand the machinery of death while working on this project. He personally described to his son the cruel professionalism of the gas chambers and the crematoria. In chilling detail, Vladek recounted the atrocities that occurred when huge numbers of Hungarian Jews entered the camp. The Nazis didn't have enough room in the crematoria and instead created giant pits where the prisoners were burned. Prisoners, both alive and dead, were placed in the pits and doused with gasoline. The horrific account made both Vladek and his son sick with grief. The extent of the Germans' inhumanity was inconceivable, yet such actions need to be remembered and retold.

## Evacuation

Because they feared the Russians were coming, the Nazis marched all of the prisoners of Auschwitz back into Germany for relocation to another camp. After the massive march, during which many prisoners died or were killed, the "citizens" of Auschwitz ended up in Germany. The next morning, they were crammed into large cattle cars so tightly that most of them couldn't move. Some could barely breathe. Typical of his resourcefulness, Vladek used a small blanket he had saved and made a sling to sit in. He attached it to some hooks on the ceiling and survived by eating snow off of the roof. He also passed snow to other prisoners, saving more lives than just his own.

The prisoners were kept in the car, some not moving for a week, until almost all the inmates were dead. They were starving and covered in their own filth. When they finally reached their new location, they learned it was Dachau, another German concentration camp. The conditions there were even worse than at Auschwitz. Vladek struggled to survive and avoid lice that spread diseases such as typhus. Hundreds of people, dead from typhus infections, were stacked in the barracks. When Vladek caught typhus, too, he had to walk across the dead just to get to a makeshift bathroom.

## Liberation

Although the prisoners didn't know it, the war was coming to a close in 1944. At Dachau one day, German soldiers began looking for POWs to exchange at the Swiss border. Because he was sick and weak, Vladek was chosen. He was put on a passenger train and brought to the Swiss border where, after a few tense moments, he was finally freed. American soldiers arrived and allowed Vladek and some others to stay at the base camp as long as they worked. The war was over. The Nazi reign had ended. For many, the loss of millions of human lives—both in the Holocaust and in combat—was too much to comprehend.

Once freed, Vladek wanted to return home. Although the Spiegelmans had been separated, Anja made it out alive as well and returned to Sosnowiec, Poland. Vladek's return journey took him throughout Germany, to refugee camps and back. He eventually

On this page of *Maus II*, Spiegelman juxtaposed his contemporary life with events from his family's past. He updated his readers about the deaths of both his mother, Anja, who committed suicide in 1968, and his father, Vladek, who died of natural causes in 1982. Although he recounted the critical and commercial success of his first book, he remained depressed and riddled with feelings of guilt and despondency.

made it back to Poland to his home and his wife. They left Poland in 1946, feeling that nothing was left for them in their home country.

## In the End

The Spiegelmans lived a nightmare that was shared by millions of European Jews during World War II. The Holocaust stripped everything from these families. Although some survived, they were never the same again. Spiegelman used *Maus* to depict how the Holocaust not only affected his father and mother, but also himself, his wife, and everyone in his family.

In a moving two-page spread at the end of *Maus II*, Vladek and his son discuss the fate of both sides of the family. In the story, they examine a box of old photographs of deceased relatives. Instead of including them as they actually appeared, Spiegelman illustrated each photo with his family members as mice. By the end of *Maus*, it is clear that Vladek had very little time left—that he would soon be joining these other family members in death. Spiegelman never sentimentalized his father's problems, but throughout *Maus*, he showed the depths of strength a normal man can possess under incredible circumstances. Despite the characters having animal faces, the comic is considered among the most successful in putting a human face on the tragedies of the Holocaust.

# CHAPTER 6

# THE *NEW YORKER* NINETIES

The start of the 1990s signaled the end of the *Maus* saga, and with it some surprises for Spiegelman. Critical appreciation for *Maus* was already widespread by the time of the completion of part one, but Spiegelman's profile within the highbrow New York art world was exploding by 1990. That same year, he was the recipient of a Guggenheim Fellowship, a prestigious financial award that would aid him in finishing *Maus*.

A fellowship is a grant of money awarded to somebody working on an important work. Art fellowships are usually reserved for studio—not comic—artists. The Guggenheim money allowed Spiegelman the freedom to work only on the projects he was truly interested in, such as *RAW*. After all, he and Françoise Mouly were parents by this point.

They had a daughter, Nadja, and a son, Dashiell, followed in 1991.

Being a parent meant having increased responsibility, and for a freelance comic artist, job security can sometimes be difficult. An artist is often forced to accept assignments that he or she would rather not do. Sometimes artists accept work based solely on the fact that they need money. Spiegelman explained the benefits of the Guggenheim grant, saying in a *St. Louis Post-Dispatch* interview, "it allowed me to say no to things. Like if somebody called me up and asked me if I would draw lots of inner tubes for some advertising material for tons of money, it was easy to say no to that. I guess you could say a Guggenheim [grant] is 'just say no' insurance."

## The Prize Winner

While it was obvious that *Maus* was successful in the ways that Spiegelman hoped, its success was made clearer when he won the 1992 Pulitzer Prize. The Pulitzer is the premier award given annually to outstanding works of journalism. Usually it is only awarded to works of hard journalism and serious literature. No comic book had ever won a Pulitzer, although many would argue that one should have. That year, the prize committee decided to honor Spiegelman with a special award for *Maus*.

The award was a tribute to Spiegelman's work, and it showed that comics can be just as important as prose or poetry. With this serious endorsement, the world finally had a comic that could sit next to Batman on the shelves of a comic-book store, next to Will Eisner in a bookstore, or in the gift shop at the Holocaust Museum in Washington, D.C. That Spiegelman's work could be considered fine art was further evidenced in a gallery exhibition of his work at New York's Museum of Modern Art (MoMA).

## The Cover Story

Following his success with *Maus*, Spiegelman needed to find his next project. He was in a respected position since he had become one of the highest profile cartoonists in the world. *RAW* was still being published, but Spiegelman wanted more. One magazine that gave him a place to do something different was the famous literary and cultural magazine, the *New Yorker*. In 1992, Spiegelman began drawing covers for it. The editor in chief, Tina Brown, was then introduced to Spiegelman's wife, Françoise Mouly. Brown hired Mouly to be the art director of the *New Yorker*, and Spiegelman joined as a consultant and cover artist.

Spiegelman remained at the *New Yorker* as a staff artist and contributing editor until 2003, when he resigned because of creative differences. At the time, the *New Yorker* covers were usually conservative, more in the tradition of twentieth-century painter Norman Rockwell than anything else. The covers were definitely not always a source of controversy. Spiegelman aimed to change those conventions. With his *New Yorker* covers, he wanted to bring the issues that he thought were important in New York to people's attention. Suddenly,

Spiegelman was a frequent cover artist, contributor, and consulting editor to the *New Yorker* magazine throughout the 1990s. Many of his cover designs for the magazine were extremely controversial, bringing a great deal of attention to the magazine during his tenure. Spiegelman left the magazine after ten years in September 2003 due to creative differences.

the magazine that had once represented the old, wealthy New York point of view suddenly featured bold, topical, and sometimes controversial covers.

One example of Spiegelman's attempt to push buttons is a 1993 cover that ran after New York's Crown Heights racial conflict. It pictured a Hasidic Jewish man kissing a black woman. Another was a 1995 cover that combined April 15, the deadline for filing income tax returns, with the Christian holiday of Good Friday, which happened to fall on the same day that year. This cover featured an Easter bunny figure crucified by tax forms. Others included a group of microphones pointed at former President Bill Clinton's pants during media coverage of his affair with White House intern Monica Lewinski. Other covers had children running around with newspaper hats that featured words such as "rape" and "murder" on them.

Spiegelman's covers reached a national audience. The *Los Angeles Times* said, "Spiegelman has become one of the *New Yorker*'s most sensational artists, in recent years drawing illustrations for covers that are meant not just to be plainly understood, but also to reach up and tattoo your eyeballs with images once unimaginable in the magazine of old moneyed taste . . ." But maybe the most effective cover of all wasn't one that could be considered controversial. After the World Trade Center towers fell on September 11, 2001, he created a simple, sober cover of dark blue with two black rectangular silhouettes representing the towers.

## Odds and Ends

While the *New Yorker* was Spiegelman's main artistic playground for much of the 1990s, he was involved with other projects and publications during the same time. He helped shape and mold the comics section of the upscale men's magazine *Details* as its comix editor, a job that allowed him to continue with the editorial work that he started with *RAW*. Spiegelman did much of the same thing for the *New York Press*, choosing the artists for its comics section. He also released a collaborative comic under the *RAW* imprint called *The Narrative Corpse*, in which different comic artists would pass the story to one another and try to continue it in whatever way they saw fit. In 1997, some of his older comics were reprinted as a book called *Breakdowns: From Maus to Now: An Anthology of Strips* named after his story about his stay in a state mental institution.

Since Spiegelman's comics were now regarded by many as respectable literature, he also tackled his labor of love—designing and illustrating a new edition of Joseph Moncure March's *The Wild Party*, a long poem set in the 1920s era of Prohibition. It was a natural fit for someone like Spiegelman who was an avid reader his entire life. Illustrating *The Wild Party* allowed him to try his hand at something a little more glamorous. Along the same lines, after taking such great pains to prove that adult comics could be popular, Spiegelman created his first children's book, *Open Me . . . I'm a Dog*.

Throughout the 1990s, Spiegelman's visibility intensified. He was, and is, considered the king of the New York cartooning world. Whether his expertise is sought to help publishers determine what kinds of comics to include in their magazines or to write an obituary for a famous cartoonist (as he did for *Spy vs. Spy* creator Antonio Prohias), Spiegelman has become the ultimate comics "go-to guy." He is among the most visible comic artists and illustrators working today.

# CHAPTER 7

# THE STATE OF THE ART

During the first years of the new millennium, Art Spiegelman has had plenty of work to keep him busy. In 2001, he and Françoise Mouly set their sights on the world of children's literature. From the birth of the comics industry, comic books had been readily available to kids. Drug stores and grocery stores were the best and easiest places to obtain such books. Although that was the way things were years ago, and the way that both Spiegelman and Mouly remembered, it was far from reality in 2001.

The 1990s were a particularly harsh time for comic books. Once a fixture of the newsstand and magazine racks, comics had become virtually invisible outside of specialty comic shops. One of the greatest threats to comics' dominance as kids' entertainment was the video game, which had become increasingly popular. A huge boom in comic sales at the dawn of the 1990s had gone bust, and the industry was reeling from the aftereffects. Kids who had been paying money for each alternate cover of a comic book were now finding that such editions had little monetary value. The notion that buying a collectible comic book could later finance one's college education had not come to fruition, and it drove the industry to its knees.

With the increasing presence and popularity of video games and the lagging sales of comics, many grocery stores and drugstores stopped selling comic books. Comics publishers were desperate to get the books back in the hands of kids but no longer had any shelf space in stores. By the year 2000, the majority of the people buying comics were adults who had been purchasing them for decades. The audience wasn't growing. It looked like comics might be headed for extinction.

## A Little Bit of Lit

By 2001, Spiegelman's two children, Nadja and Dashiell, were thirteen and nine, respectively. They had discovered their dad's vast collection of classic comic books and would often spend hours looking them over. Watching his own children discover the joy of comics was inspiring to Spiegelman, and it awakened him to comics' potential as a teaching aid. "Comics are really one of the best ways of teaching a kid how to read," he said in an interview with *New York Times* writer Karen McPhearson. "Kids don't think of comics as medicine.

And comics also offer a more lucid kind of storytelling than many other types of kids' books."

Coupled with his own kids' interest in comics was Spiegelman's own disgust at what he perceived to be boring and conservative children's literature. Unhappy with mainstream children's literature, Spiegelman and Mouly cooked up an idea. While Spiegelman had already created a children's book, *Open Me . . . I'm a Dog*, this new idea united Spiegelman and Mouly's love for comics and traditional children's fairy tales. Their new project, *Little Lit*, debuted in 2000. *Little Lit*'s first edition, subtitled *Folklore & Fairy Tale Funnies*, contained twelve children's fairy tales done in a comic style. Most of the stories are adaptations of old fairy tales, such as "Humpty Dumpty" and "Sleeping Beauty," with some artists like former *Daredevil* artist David Mazzuchelli tackling lesser-known ethnic stories. Spiegelman himself adapted an old Hasidic Jewish story called "Prince Rooster." *Little Lit* even included a reprint of a 1943 version of "The Gingerbread Man" by *Pogo* legend Walt Kelly, a Disney animator and one of Spiegelman's boyhood heroes.

One of the main goals of the *Little Lit* series, in addition to making fun, quality children's literature, was to create children's comics that parents could also enjoy. Parents, after all, were reading the stories to the kids. Many of the stories in *Little Lit* have a darker tone than would normally be found in children's books, but Spiegelman didn't see this as a problem. After all, the original versions of the Grimm brothers' fairy tales were often much more grisly than the ones people are familiar

a Hasidic parable

The comic drawing shown here of a rooster is the opening page of a Hasidic parable that appeared in the first *Little Lit* anthology, *Folklore & Fairy Tale Funnies* (2000). With the help of his wife, Françoise Mouly, Spiegelman contacted some of the finest illustrators and cartoonists working today to retell classic fairy tales in a contemporary format. Chip Kidd designed the stunning book, which also includes a unique board game created by Chris Ware (*Jimmy Corrigan: The Smartest Kid on Earth*).

with today. Having proved that comics could be serious literature for adults with *Maus*, it was time for Spiegelman to bring comics back into the hands of children. "It was like finally some people were going, 'Yes! Comics are for adults,' and here we were kind of stupidly parading out into the battle zone going, 'Yeah, but wait, wait, comics aren't just for adults anymore,'" he explained in a 2003 article in *Time* magazine.

Making the new fairy-tale books appealing to adults didn't end with the content, though. The books themselves may have been comics, but Spiegelman and Mouly made sure that they were also beautifully produced and appealing. The thick, hardback volume came equipped with a board game, Fairy Tale Road Rage, designed by *Acme Novelty Library*'s Chris Ware. The book was designed by Spiegelman and award-winning designer Chip Kidd. It was created to look as good on someone's coffee table as it would in the hands of an interested child.

*Folklore & Fairy Tale Funnies* was successful, appearing regularly on children's book bestseller lists. Soon, two more volumes of *Little Lit* followed. In 2001, Spiegelman and Mouly released *Strange Stories for Strange Kids*, and in 2003, *It Was a Dark and Silly Night*. The main concept in *Silly Night* is that every story in the book must begin with the words, "It was a dark and silly night." Creators like *Sandman*'s Neil Gaiman, Lemony Snicket, and William Joyce contributed. The *Little Lit* series may have started as two concerned parents' effort to make quality children's comics, but it ended up being much more, fitting in perfectly with Spiegelman's ongoing crusade to prove that comic illustration is both simple yet sophisticated enough for everyone.

## Plastic Fantastic

Spiegelman's obsession with the history of comic art led him to discover many forgotten artists whose worth was equal to or greater than that of many of the more popular artists. One such artist was Jack Cole, the creator of Plastic Man, a wisecracking superhero who could stretch and transform his body into almost any shape. Cole, who committed suicide in 1958, was largely forgotten despite being one of the best comic artists of his time. His *Plastic Man* series was extremely popular. Plastic Man was popular enough to have his own television cartoon at one point, and is the star of a new series for DC Comics and a member of DC's Justice League of America alongside Superman, Batman, and Wonder Woman. His creator, however, was not so recognizable.

Because he so admired Cole's work, Spiegelman wrote an article about Cole for the *New Yorker* in 1999 called "Forms Stretched to Their Limits." The article blossomed into something much larger in 2001, when Spiegelman got together with his *Little Lit* co-designer Chip Kidd to expand the piece into a full-blown book. The book, *Jack Cole and Plastic Man: Forms Stretched to Their Limits*, is a homage to an artist the world was in danger of forgetting. Spiegelman and Kidd were highly praised for their work. While it didn't feature any of Spiegelman's work, the book showcased his journalistic skills, which had been displayed earlier in *Maus*.

## Living in the Shadow

During his career, Spiegelman has used a strong fusion of comics and journalism. And while it was on display in *Maus* as well as many of Spiegelman's other comics, it

In 2002, Spiegelman devoted his time to a more topical comic piece, *In the Shadow of No Towers*, an ongoing response to the terrorist attacks on September 11, 2001, that first appeared in the *Forward* in 2002, a progressive Jewish newspaper. Spiegelman has since been more interested in addressing politics and current events in his art, something that he wasn't always able to do in other projects.

revealed itself in its strongest form in the artist's most recent project, a comic strip called *In the Shadow of No Towers*. People throughout the United States were devastated by the terrorist attacks on the World Trade Center and the Pentagon on September 11, 2001. Spiegelman had spent almost his entire life in New York City, and the attacks affected him and his family very deeply.

The Spiegelman family lives only blocks away from where the World Trade Center once stood in lower Manhattan. When the first plane struck the Twin Towers, Spiegelman and Mouly were walking down the street. Their children were at school and in the chaos,

Spiegelman had to find his daughter and son, not sure if they were hurt.

Spiegelman's parents, as Holocaust survivors, had brought him up with a pronounced sense of impending danger. "I grew up being told by my [Holocaust] survivor parents that the world is an incredibly dangerous place and I should always be prepared to flee," he explained in an interview with Alana Newhouse in a 2002 issue of the *Forward* newspaper. Finding himself amid the life-threatening danger of the terrorist attacks severely damaged his state of mind. The months that followed the attacks were torturous for Spiegelman, and he found himself, as he explained in the *Foward* newspaper, "more or less trapped in September 11."

The solution for Spiegelman was the same as it had always been during times of stress: he decided to create a comic book about the attacks. He believed he could help himself and his fellow New Yorkers better cope with the tragedy. It was a return to waters that he hadn't swam in for quite a while. Aside from *Little Lit*, Spiegelman had been concentrating most of his time on covers for the *New Yorker* and other illustrations, as well as editing. As he got older and had less time, creating comics was an activity that had fallen by the wayside. The attacks, however, revitalized his energy as a comic artist. "September 11 forced me to take inventory of everything left in my brain," he said in an interview in the *Forward*. "Over the past few years I had stopped doing comics because they were too hard." After what happened, though, he saw no other alternative but to use all of his talents. He continued, "I made a vow as we all huddled safely that day, in the shadow of no towers, that I would draw comics again."

*In the Shadow of No Towers* is presented in a completely different form than Spiegelman, or anyone else, usually used. Instead of a series of panels moving in a traditional left-to-right horizontal orientation, Spiegelman created *Shadow* on a large newspaper-sized broadsheet, a style that hasn't been seen in the United States since the beginning of the twentieth century. The format allowed him to design the entire page. Instead of one single story, its panels dealt with various issues all over the page. The reader's eye can glance over whatever catches his or her interest. In addition to the main subject, smaller panels throughout the page focus on different issues. For instance, one panel addresses the recent ban on cigarette smoking in New York City bars and restaurants by Mayor Michael Bloomberg. The single-page format also appealed to Spiegelman for a darker reason that really expressed his fear. "If I thought in page units," he explained in the October 15, 2003, *New York Times*, "I might live long enough to do another page."

Since he was working for the *New Yorker*, it seemed logical that this new work would appear there, but Spiegelman had other plans. *Shadow* is different from Spiegelman's other work in another important way. The content of *Shadow* is extremely political, perhaps more so than anything else he has ever produced. Many of the cartoons equally take to task both Muslim extremists and the administration of President George W. Bush. One page, for example, features a sleeping Spiegelman (again pictured as a

Art Spiegelman as he appeared at the New York Is Book Country Festival in September 2003. At the time, Spiegelman debuted the third edition of *Little Lit*, the collaborative young adult book series that he created with his wife, Françoise Mouly, to eager fans. *Little Lit: It Was A Dark and Silly Night* features the work of many well-known and some up-and-coming cartoonists and illustrators.

mouse), sitting at his drafting table with evil, grinning caricatures of both Osama bin Laden and President Bush, each armed with weapons.

Upset and concerned that the mainstream media in the United States have become weakened, timid, and more conservative since the terrorist attacks, Spiegelman published *Shadow* through *Forward*, a Jewish newspaper, and in European papers like the German *Die Zeit* and the *London Review of Books*. The newspapers are more progressive, and Spiegelman had the freedom to say whatever was on his mind without worrying about the censorship that may come with a more mainstream publication. As a result, *Shadow* hadn't been read by many Americans until it was published by Random House in 2004. Called a love letter to the city of New York by critics, *Shadow* received praise for its provocative tone. In October 2004, it reached number six on the New York Times Bestseller list.

## The Art of Being Art

Spiegelman has worked steadily in comics for almost four decades. During that time, he has always followed his heart and his conscience to create work that's both personal and political. Through his positions as an editor and teacher, he has done perhaps more than any other comic artist to draw attention to an art form that is in constant danger of extinction. He has discovered and mentored many budding cartoonists. Most important, *Maus* and the publicity that came with its Pulitzer Prize have helped to convince people in serious literary circles that comics can be every bit as important as any other literary work. Spiegelman's contributions to the medium place him comfortably on the list of cartoonists that he so greatly admires. As for what else he has to say, who knows? Keep your eyes on the funny pages.

The End

# SELECTED WORKS

*Breakdowns: From Maus to Now: An Anthology of Strips.* New York: Belier Press, 1977.

*In the Shadow of No Towers.* New York: Pantheon, 2004.

*Jack Cole and Plastic Man: Forms Stretched to Their Limits* (with Chip Kidd). San Francisco: Chronicle Books, 2001.

*Little Lit: Folklore Fairy Tale Funnies.* Edited by Art Spiegelman with Françoise Mouly. New York: HarperCollins, 2000.

*Little Lit: It Was a Dark and Silly Night.* Edited by Art Spiegelman with Françoise Mouly. New York: HarperCollins, 2003.

*Little Lit: Strange Stories For Strange Kids.* Edited by Art Spiegelman with Françoise Mouly. New York: HarperCollins, 2001.

*Maus I: A Survivor's Tale: My Father Bleeds History.* New York: Pantheon, 1986.

*Maus II: A Survivor's Tale: And Here My Troubles Began.* New York: Pantheon, 1992.

*The Narrative Corpse: A Chain Story by 69 Artists!.* Edited by Art Spiegelman and R. Sikoryak. Richmond, Virginia: Raw Books, 1995.

*RAW,* Volumes 1–8. Edited by Art Spiegelman with Françoise Mouly. Richmond, Virginia: Raw Books, 1980–1991.

*Read Yourself Raw.* Edited by Art Spiegelman with Françoise Mouly. New York: Pantheon, 1987.

# SELECTED AWARDS

## Comic-Con International Inkpot Award

Best Comic Anthology (*RAW*, 1987)

## Guggenheim Fellowship (1990)

## Harvey Award

Best Anthology (*RAW*, 1991)

Best Graphic Album of Previous Published Material
(*Maus II: A Survivor's Tale: And Here My Troubles Began*, 1992)

Best Biographical, Historical, or Journalistic Presentation (*Jack Cole and Plastic Man: Forms Stretched to Their Limits*, with Chip Kidd), 2002.

## Los Angeles Times Book Prize

*Maus I: A Survivor's Tale: My Father Bleeds History*, 1993

## National Foundation for Jewish Culture, Jewish Cultural Achievement Award

Best Visual Artist, 1996

## Pulitzer Prize

Special Award and Citation (*Maus I: A Survivor's Tale: My Father Bleeds History*, 1992)

## Will Eisner Comic Industry Award

Best Graphic Album-Reprint (*Maus II: A Survivor's Tale: And Here My Troubles Began*, 1992)

# GLOSSARY

**anti-Semitism** Hostility toward or discrimination against Jews as a religious, ethnic, or racial group.

**atrocity** A repulsive or loathsome condition or state.

**conglomerate** A business corporation made up of different companies that operate in diversified fields.

**dogmatic** Marked by an authoritarian, often arrogant assertion of principles.

**Final Solution** The Nazi program for the extermination (murder) of all the Jews in Europe.

**ghetto** A section of a city in which an ethnic or economically depressed minority group is restricted, as by poverty or social pressure.

**highbrow** Relating to one who has or affects superior learning or culture.

**indelible** Incapable of being removed, erased, or washed away.

**metaphor** A figure of speech in which a term that ordinarily designates an object or idea is used to designate a dissimilar object or idea in order to suggest comparison or analogy.

**pacifist** A person who is opposed to war and violence of all kinds.

**parody** A satirical imitation, as of a literary or musical work.

**quirk** A characteristic of a person or a thing that is odd or offbeat.

**refugee** One who flees to find refuge from oppression or persecution.

**resurgence** Rising or tending to rise again; making a comeback.

**satirical** A word describing something that is ironic.

*selektion* A process used by the Nazis at death camps to separate prisoners into two groups: those who could work (and therefore continue to live) and those who could not (and would be immediately killed).

**stereotype** A conventional and usually oversimplified conception or belief.

**typhus** Any of various bacterial diseases caused by body lice and marked by a high fever, stupor, delirium, headache, and a dark-red rash.

**typography** The style, arrangement, or appearance of typeset matter.

# FOR MORE INFORMATION

**The Comics Journal**
7563 Lake City Way NE
Seattle, WA 98115
(800) 657-1100 or (206) 524-1967
e-mail: fbicomix@fantagraphics.com
Web site: http://www.tcj.com

**New York City Comic Book Museum**
P.O. Box 230676
New York, NY 10023
(212) 712-9454
e-mail: nyccbm@hotmail.com
Web site: http://www.nyccomicbookmuseum.org

## Web Sites

Due to the changing nature of Internet links, the
Rosen Publishing Group, Inc., has developed an online
list of Web sites related to the subject of this book.
This site is updated regularly. Please use this link to
access the list:

http://www.rosenlinks.com/lgn/arsp

# FOR FURTHER READING

Spiegelman, Art. *Maus: A Survivor's Tale: Part One: My Father Bleeds History*. New York: Pantheon Books, 1986.

Spiegelman, Art. *Maus: A Survivor's Tale: Part Two: And Here My Troubles Began*. New York: Pantheon Books, 1991.

Spiegelman, Art and Chip Kidd. *Jack Cole and Plastic Man: Forms Stretched to Their Limits*. San Francisco, CA: Chronicle Books, 2001.

Spiegelman, Art and Françoise Mouly. *Little Lit: Folklore & Fairy Tale Funnies*. New York: Harpercollins Juvenile Books, 2000.

Spiegelman, Art and Françoise Mouly. *Little Lit: It Was a Dark and Silly Night*. New York: Harpercollins Juvenile Books, 2003.

Spiegelman, Art and Françoise Mouly. *Little Lit: Strange Stories for Strange Kids*. New York: Harpercollins Juvenile Books, 2001.

# BIBLIOGRAPHY

Bird, Alan. "Comic Books Come of Age." bookpage.com. Retrieved February 27, 2004 (http://www.bookpage.com/0308bp/spiegelman_mouly.html).

Bolhafner, Stephen J. "Comix as Art: The Man Behind the 'Maus.'" *St. Louis Post-Dispatch*, June 23, 1991.

Groth, Gary. "Art Spiegelman." tcj.com. Retrieved February 10, 2004 (http://www.tcj.com/2_archives/i_spiegelman.html).

Gussow, Mel. "Dark Nights, Sharp Pens." *New York Times*, October 15, 2003.

MacPherson, Karen. "Comic Book Styles Come of Age (Again)." Post-Gazette.com. January 9, 2001. Retrieved March 1, 2004 (http://postgazette.com/books/20010109corner2.asp).

Newhouse, Alana. "The Paranoids Were Right." Forward.com. Retrieved October 15, 2003 (http://www.forward.com/issues/2002/02.09.06/arts1.html).

Pratt, Rob. "The 'Maus' That Roared." metroactive.com. Retrieved March 1, 2004 (http://www.metroactive.com/papers/cruz/10.06.99/spiegelman-9940.html).

Rall, Ted. "The King of Comix." villagevoice.com. Retrieved February 11, 2004 (http://www.villagevoice.com/issues/9930/rall.php).

Spiegelman, Art. *Maus II: A Survivor's Tale: And Here My Troubles Began.* New York: Pantheon Books, 1991.

Spiegelman, Art. *Maus I: A Survivor's Tale: My Father Bleeds History.* New York: Pantheon Books, 1986.

# INDEX

## About the Author

Tom Forget has been enjoying comics since before he could read. He prefers Zap! Bang! Boom! superhero comics, but grudgingly admits that these smarty-pants graphic novels are pretty great, too. He lives in Brooklyn with a girl and a dog.

## Credits

Cover, p. 44 © Jacques M. Chenet/Corbis. Used with permission of Art Spiegelman; p. 4–5 © Ted Streshinsky/Corbis; p. 11 © Bettmann/Corbis; p. 13 © Jacques M. Chenet/Corbis; p. 16 SPIDER-MAN: TM & © 2004 Marvel Characters, Inc. Used with permission; p. 24 copyright © Robert Crumb, 1967; pp. 29, 59, 63, 67, 68, 73 From MAUS I: A SURVIVOR'S TALE/MY FATHER BLEEDS HISTORY by Art Spiegelman, copyright © 1973, 1980, 1981, 1982, 1984, 1985, 1986 by Art Spiegelman. Used by permission of Pantheon Books, a division of Random House, Inc.; pp. 30, 38, 95 © Art Spiegelman. Reproduced with permission; p. 33 © 1978 Will Eisner Studios, Inc.; p. 41 © 1986 TOPPS Chewing Gum, Inc.; p. 49 United States Holocaust Memorial Museum; p. 53 photo by Cindy Reiman for The Rosen Publishing Group; pp. 75, 78 (top and bottom), 81, 84 From MAUS II: A SURVIVOR'S TALE/AND HERE MY TROUBLES BEGAN by Art Spiegelman, copyright © 1986, 1989, 1990, 1991 by Art Spiegelman. Used by permission of Pantheon Books, a division of Random House, Inc.; p. 89 Art Spiegelman/*The New Yorker*. Copyright © 1996 Condé Nast Publications Inc. Reprinted by permission. All Rights Reserved; p. 98 From IN THE SHADOW OF NO TOWERS by Art Spiegelman, copyright © 2004 by Art Spiegelman. Used by permission of Pantheon Books, a division of Random House, Inc.; p. 101 © Cindy Reiman.

Designer: Les Kanturek; Editor: Joann Jovinelly